DESTINATION
MARS

S.K. Das is Honorary Advisor to the Indian Space Research Organisation and the author of a number of books including *Mission Moon: Exploring the Moon with Chandrayaan 1* and *All About Rockets*.

DESTINATION MARS

SECRETS OF THE
RED PLANET REVEALED

S.K. DAS

RED TURTLE
RUPA

Published in Red Turtle by
Rupa Publications India Pvt. Ltd. 2013
7/16, Ansari Road, Daryaganj
New Delhi 110002

Sales Centres:

Allahabad Bengaluru Chennai
Hyderabad Jaipur Kathmandu
Kolkata Mumbai

ISBN: 978-81-291-2939-0

10 9 8 7 6 5 4 3 2 1

The moral right of the author has been asserted.

Printed at Thomson Press India Ltd., Faridabad

For the ISRO family, past and present,
who have striven to conquer space

Contents

Foreword

India's tryst with space science dates back to our ancient astronomers and mathematicians who have striven to understand our place in the Universe. Now, in the 21st century, we stand at a unique time in our exploration of the heavens.

Robotic probes have found traces of water on Mars and pointed to the possibility of oceans underlying Jupiter's moons. Astronomers are discovering more planets, and these findings indicate that our Universe may be more habitable than previously known. Worldwide, the exploratory voyages of the next few decades have the potential — within our lifetimes — to answer many age-old questions.

Mars with its many similarities to Earth is an important mission prospective for the Indian Space Research Organisation (ISRO). Our Mars Orbiter will take almost 300 days to reach the intended Martian orbit, and the long flight of the craft through space is indeed challenging. This will prove ISRO's technological capability of sending a spacecraft so deep into space. It is also a science mission because it is designed to carry out observations of the physical features of Mars and do a study of the Martian atmosphere with five scientific payloads. It paves the way for the scientific community to take a look at Mars from close quarters.

Shri S. K. Das' book *Destination Mars* is a welcome and timely development. It tells the story of Mars as it captured the imagination of people in the early days, first as a red object in the sky with its eccentric motion, and later as a planet where people thought life might have existed in a similar form as on Earth. The book also tells us how these misconceptions and illusions were proved wrong when spacecraft probing Mars sent back pictures of the Red Planet. The book also provides details of ISRO's mission to Mars proposed in October 2013.

Destination Mars has been written for the young readers of India. The language is lucid and easy to understand. The pictures and diagrams included here will help young minds appreciate the various facets of space exploration and of Mars as a planet. I am sure this will be an useful companion not only for students sparking their interest in space science and space journeys but also for others interested in interplanetary exploration.

K. Radhakrishnan
Chairman, Indian Space Research Organisation
Bangalore

Introduction

The soldiers of ancient Rome followed a rigorous training drill. Every morning they would march to a field just outside Rome and train for hours. The field where they trained was named after the planet Mars. There was a reason for that. Mars was the Roman god of war and it was believed that he had never lost a war.

The ancient Greeks and Romans called Mars the Red Planet because it appeared in the night sky as a star bathed in the colour of blood. This led the ancients to equate Mars with war and aggression. People thought of it with awe. Every time they looked up at the night sky and saw a blood-red dot moving ominously from west to east, they were filled with fear.

They also found it strange that at certain times, Mars behaved in a suspicious manner. All of a sudden, it would change direction and move from east to west. It was as if it was making an abrupt hairpin turn and heading in the opposite direction. And then, a couple of months later, it would make another hairpin turn and resume its journey from west to east.

To them, Mars resembled an angry warrior whose behaviour was erratic and unpredictable. Did the planet really stop, go backward for days, change its mind and then continue to move forward? Or was it just a ploy to surprise an enemy up there and waylay it?

After the telescope was invented, astronomers could peer at Mars and study it a bit more closely. The planet changed colour in different seasons. There were huge dust storms that swept the plains and darkened the entire planet for days. It had white polar caps, which grew quickly in winter and almost disappeared in summer. The astronomers also saw several straight lines criss-crossing the planet's surface. These lines joined greenish areas that looked as if they were covered by vegetation.

This led to the birth of a fascinating idea. It was thought that the straight lines were canals built by Martians to carry water for watering their plants. During summer in the southern hemisphere of Mars, the polar ice would melt and provide running water to the rest of the planet through a big network of canals built by an ancient, intelligent and technologically advanced race of Martians. As the summer progressed on Mars, the canals would fill up and the plants would get water and blossom, making them visible to humans on Earth.

This idea grew and prospered and led to further theories. If the Martian race was not only warlike but intelligent too, should we fear an invasion from these Martians? An American radio play in 1938 convinced people that creatures from Mars had actually landed on Earth in their war machines. There was panic in the United States. Hundreds of thousands of people hid themselves or ran away from their homes. Almost the entire nation was convinced that Martians had invaded their country.

Of course, the whole thing was just a joke. Once space probes were invented and sent to Mars over the last fifty years, pictures taken by these probes showed that no such canals exist there. There is no sign of life—plants or intelligent Martians—on the planet. Mars is a very cold, dry planet where liquid water cannot exist on the surface.

Scientists have now discovered that Mars is even more complex than they thought it was. It is peppered with craters and cut by canyons deep enough to swallow the Earth's Grand Canyon. It has the tallest volcano in the solar system. There are large, dry channels on the surface which indicate that once there was running water on the Martian surface.

This means Mars was once wetter and warmer, and conditions for life existed at some point of time in the Martian history. Scientists also point to pieces of Mars that are to be found on Earth. These are stones from the surface of Mars that were thrown out as a result of some impact and landed on Earth as meteorites. These stones have grains that are mineral formations similar to formations produced on Earth by certain organisms living in seas. Scientists believe that this could be evidence pointing to the possible existence of life early in the history of Mars. Was there liquid water on the Martian surface? Did life ever begin on the Red Planet? We need to know much more about Mars to answer these questions.

We are well on the way to discovering more and more about Mars. Countries have been sending space probes to the Red Planet for fifty years now, and within another twenty years perhaps humans will visit it too. A lot has been learnt from these space probes but there is still a lot more to learn. For that reason, we have to keep on exploring Mars. Such exploration is important because it is as much about Earth and its origins as it is about Mars.

India is sending a mission to Mars in October 2013 or so. Our country will send many more missions, and one day, Indians will land on Mars and explore it. How we land on Mars and what we do there will depend on the space scientists of tomorrow, many of whom may be from among you, the readers. This book is for you.

1
All About the Red Planet

How was the solar system born?

About five billion years ago, a number of old stars died. It is difficult to think of stars dying, but they do. These stars left behind a giant cloud of gas and dust. The cloud was so big that it spread across about 24 trillion kilometres.

An explosion of a nearby star caused a disturbance that sent ripples through the cloud. The ripples stirred the gas and dust particles in the cloud, making them come close to each other. There was gravitational attraction now, and the gas and dust particles began to clump together and interact. The interaction made them spin faster and faster, and as the cloud spun, it flattened into a disk.

In 10 million years, the material at the centre of the disk became the Sun. Much of the remaining material in the disk, particularly the heavier gases, travelled to the outer region of the disk. They formed the planets Jupiter, Saturn, Uranus and Neptune. These four planets are called gas giants because they are made up mostly of gas. Their atmosphere is very thick and dense. They have solid cores but they do not have solid surfaces. It will be difficult to walk or ride a bicycle or drive a car on these gas giants. These planets are really big. For example, 318 Earths can easily fit inside Jupiter.

Closer to the Sun, the remaining light gases mixed with heavier materials to form dust and ice particles that became rocks and boulders. Over a period of time, they formed the four rocky planets in the inner solar system — Mercury, Venus, Earth and Mars. These four are relatively small in size.

Earth, which has a diameter of less than 13,000 kilometres, is the largest among these four planets.

Out of these four planets, Mercury is the closest to the Sun. It gets the full blast of the Sun's heat and daytime temperatures on it reach 450 degrees Celsius. It is a harsh and hostile planet, and if you are looking for another planet to settle in, Mercury is certainly not the place you should think of.

The other three planets enjoy a more soothing heat from the Sun. They are all rocky planets and broadly similar in their composition and surface conditions.

Why is Mars called the Red Planet?

Mars is the most Earth-like of all the planets in the solar system in its size and composition. But, instead of the blue oceans and green land that we have on Earth, Mars always has a red tint. That is why it is called the Red Planet. The soil on Mars is rich in iron, and oxidation of the iron gives the planet its red colour. This process of oxidation happens when a metal gets covered with a coating of oxide and becomes rusty. When anything made of iron is exposed to the elements like rain or air, it begins to rust and that is what happens on the planet Mars.

What does Mars look like when you see it from Earth?

Mars is the only planet in the solar system that we can see with the naked eye. If you are looking through a telescope, the surface features of Mars look very small, and the difference between the light and dark areas are so slight that all you see is the red colour of the planet.

If you are looking at Mars at the same time on consecutive nights, you will see almost the same side of Mars. That is because the length of a day on Mars and Earth are almost the same. A day on Mars is 24 hours and 39 minutes long, a little more than a day on Earth. This difference in the period of rotation of these two planets makes it look as if Mars is rotating slowly. Because of this difference, you can see Mars exactly at the same place after a period of forty days.

Of course, you cannot miss the ice caps in the polar regions of Mars. Earth, too, has white polar caps. But those on Mars are much smaller and thinner, and the size of these ice caps grows and recedes with the change of seasons. They grow quickly in winter and almost disappear in summer. They are also much colder than the polar caps on Earth. They contain frozen carbon dioxide as well as water ice.

Does Mars orbit around the Sun in a circle or an ellipse?

All the planets in the solar system orbit the Sun. The orbit paths are in the shape of ellipses. An ellipse looks like a circle that has been squashed slightly. It is like an oval, or like an egg. When a planet orbits in an ellipse, it moves faster when it is close to the object it is orbiting and slower when it is farther away. Since the orbit of Mars is elliptical too, its distance from the Sun is different at different points along its orbit, and this affects the visibility of Mars as seen from Earth.

Although both Earth and Mars orbit the Sun, Earth is closer to the Sun, and therefore races along its orbit more quickly. Earth makes two trips around the Sun in about the same amount of time that Mars takes to make one trip. So, sometimes Earth catches up with Mars, passes close to it and overtakes it, and at other times, the two planets are on opposite sides of the Sun, very far apart.

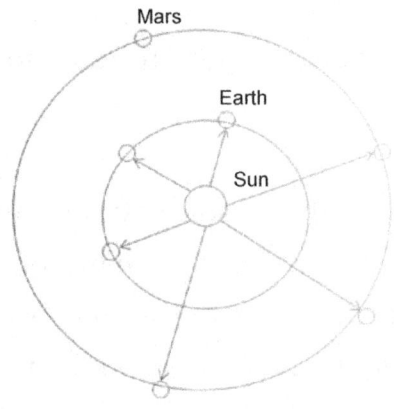

When they are on opposite sides of the Sun

What is retrograde motion?

If you look at the eastern sky at the same time each night and note where Mars appears to be compared to the constellations, you would find the planet a little farther east with each viewing. It means that Mars is moving from west to east from one night to the next. But every two years or so, there are two months during which Mars appears to be moving from east to west.

Does Mars change its direction? It looks as if while moving across the night sky, Mars makes a hairpin turn and heads in the opposite direction, and a couple of months later, it makes another hairpin turn and resumes its journey from west to east. In the olden times, people found this strange behaviour of the planet very puzzling.

Today, we know what really happens. It is caused by the ways in which Earth and Mars orbit the Sun. This change of direction in Mars' journey is only an optical illusion. It is like the illusion we have when we look out of the window of a train just as the train on the other railway track goes ahead. For a moment we feel as if our train is moving backwards. After they have passed, the two trains look like they are moving in the same direction once again. Exactly the same thing happens when Earth overtakes Mars.

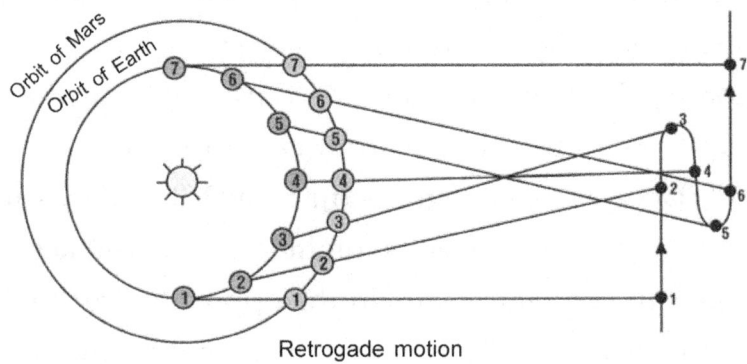

Retrogade motion

About every twenty-six months, Earth comes up from behind and overtakes Mars. While we are passing by the Red Planet, it looks to us as though Mars is going backwards. As Earth moves ahead in its orbit, we see Mars from a different angle. Then the illusion disappears and we once again see Mars moving in the right direction. This apparent erratic movement of Mars is called retrograde motion.

What is opposition?

Mars is in opposition when it is opposite the Sun in the sky as viewed from Earth. At this time Mars is closest to Earth. During opposition, Mars and the Sun are on directly opposite sides of Earth. At such times, Mars rises in the east just as the Sun is setting in the west, and then, after staying up in the sky the entire night, it sets in the west just as the Sun is rising in the east.

Opposition of Mars happens every twenty-six months. When it happens while Mars is closest to the Sun, it is called perihelic opposition. Perihelic oppositions occur every fifteen or seventeen years. At the time of perihelic opposition, Mars comes the closest to Earth. But these planets do not have perfectly stable orbits. Gravitational pull by other planets changes the shapes of these orbits quite a bit. In the case of Mars, the giant planet Jupiter influences the orbit of Mars. Therefore, some oppositions bring Mars and Earth closer together than others. At that time, Mars appears to be very bright when viewed from Earth. In fact, it becomes the brightest object in the night sky and is noticed not only by astronomers looking through telescopes but also by ordinary people who are watching the night sky.

In recent history, this kind of close encounter happened on 28 August 2003. On that day, Mars was so bright that some people thought it was the warning light of a relay station. That day Mars came closer to Earth than it had ever come in the past 60,000 years. The last time Mars came closer than this to Earth was on 12 September 57617 BC. The next time Mars will be as close or closer to Earth will be on 27 August 2287. That day is certainly worth waiting for!

2
Mars Through the Ages

The story of Mangal

In our mythology, the planet Mars is called Mangal. It is considered a fiery planet and is symbolized by the colour red. Mangal is regarded as the commander-in-chief of the heavenly army and is said to rule over blood. Mangal is described as having four arms, each arm carrying a trident, a mace, a lotus and a spear. He is shown sitting on a ram.

Our scriptures tell an interesting story about how Mangal was born. Andhakasura, a demon, had been given a boon. The boon was that if the demon got injured in war, another Andhakasura would arise from each drop of his blood that falls on earth. As a result the demon was nearly undefeatable in war.

Armed with this boon, Andhakasura started harassing the gods and sages. These gods went to Lord Shiva and begged him to kill the demon. Lord Shiva fought with the demon at Avanti, the present-day Ujjain in the state of Madhya Pradesh. But, because the demon had the boon, the war was prolonged.

Lord Shiva then wiped his brow and some sweat fell on the ground, giving birth to Mangal. The Lord now hurled his trident at the heart of the demon. The blood that streamed out was drunk by Mangal, and he did not allow a single drop to fall to the ground and Andhakasura was killed.

Ares in Greek mythology

For the ancient Greeks, Mars was Ares, the god of war. He was the son of Zeus, the supreme God and his wife Hera. The parents did not particularly like their son Ares. As Homer wrote in the *Iliad*, this was because Ares was bloodthirsty and full of wrath, yet a chicken-hearted coward.

The Greeks called the moving points of light in the sky 'planetes' or wanderers. This is the basis for the word planet. The retrograde motion of Mars set the ancient Greeks thinking. Mars would sometimes appear to move backwards and then forward, making it appear as if it was revolving around the Earth in a circular motion. On the basis of this, Ptolemy, the great Greek astronomer, proposed that Earth was at the centre of the Universe. This is known as the geocentric view of the world that held sway for the next 1,500 years.

What the scientists and astronomers said

Nicolaus Copernicus

The Christian church supported the geocentric view of the world. The Church even turned it into a dogma and punished people who dared oppose it. It was only in 1543 AD that Nicolaus Copernicus, the Polish astronomer, suggested that the solar system has the Sun at its centre. Although this discovery was pathbreaking, Copernicus was afraid of the Church and did not publish his book. When the book was finally published after his death, the Church banned the book.

The retrograde motion of Mars was the basis on which Ptolemy had proposed the geocentric view of the world. Fifteen hundred years later, it was Mars which provided the basis for explaining how planets moved. It was not the retrograde motion of Mars this time, but its elliptical orbit.

Johannes Kepler

Johannes Kepler, a German astronomer, was fascinated by Copernicus' idea of a solar system with the Sun at its centre. Kepler was working for Tycho Brahe, a Danish mathematician. Brahe was a difficult man. He had fought with his superiors and even lost half his nose in a duel. But he was a brilliant man who could build instruments to take precise measurements of the position of planets. He had spent several years measuring the position and movements of Mars.

After Brahe died, Kepler used his measurements of Mars to confirm Copernicus' idea that Earth was not the centre of the Universe. Kepler came to the conclusion that not only Mars orbited the Sun, but it did so in an elliptical manner. Brahe's measurements were so precise that they helped Kepler find out how the planets actually moved. So, Mars was the means through which the nature of planetary motion, and ultimately, the nature of gravity was discovered.

What they saw—the discovery of Mars with the telescope

The telescope was invented in 1610. Francesco Fontana, an Italian astronomer, prepared the first drawing of the Martian surface with the help of a telescope. After Fontana sketched the surface of Mars, many other astronomers did the same using their telescopes. These astronomers saw dark patches on the surface, which they drew as smudgy outlines.

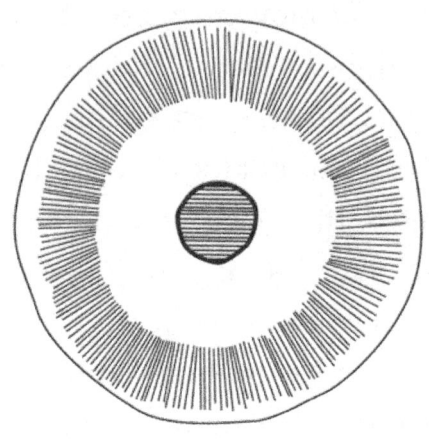

Sketch made by Francesco Fontana in 1636

Christiaan Huygens was the first one to make a sketch of Mars with details that could be identified. In his sketch, there is a dark area shaped like the letter V in the middle of the round disk of Mars. This was called the Hourglass Sea, and later renamed as Syrtis Major. Huygens also observed a very bright spot on Mars. It was the white and shining ice cap in the polar region of Mars. By watching this bright spot regularly, Hyugens measured the period of rotation of Mars. He put it at 24 hours.

Sketch made by Christiaan Huygens in 1659

In 1660, Domenico Cassini observed Mars and prepared sketches. His sketches were like paintings and did not provide any details. But he tried to calculate the period of rotation of Mars and put it at 24 hours and 40 minutes. This was more accurate than Huygens' calculation. Cassini also observed a star dimming even before Mars could cover it. This led Cassini to conclude that Mars had a substantial atmosphere, which had caused the dimming of the star.

Sketch made by Domenico Cassini in 1666

Giacomo Maraldi, Cassini's nephew, made detailed observation of Mars for forty-seven years. He observed dark areas on the surface of Mars. He also saw white caps in the polar region which grew, shrank and even disappeared at times. Maraldi concluded that Mars had four seasons of spring, summer, autumn and winter.

In the later part of the eighteenth century, there was great improvement in the quality of telescopes. William Herschel, the British astronomer, built a giant 36-inch reflecting telescope in 1777. On the basis of his observation

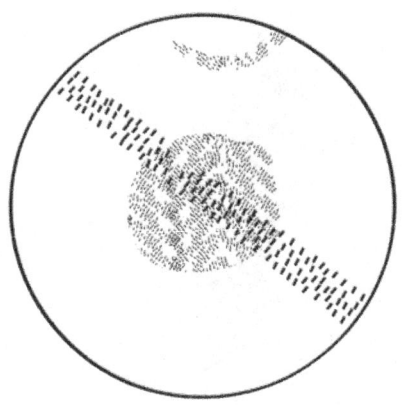

Sketch made by Giacomo Maraldi in 1719

of Mars, he calculated the period of rotation of the planet at 24 hours 39 minutes and 21.67 seconds.

Herschel also determined the tilt of Mars' axis. He put it at 28.7 degrees while the actual tilt is 25 degrees. According to Herschel, the ice caps in the polar region of Mars were composed of water ice just like ice caps in Earth's polar region. He also pointed out that the atmosphere on Mars was not very thick. All these similarities made Herschel argue that the conditions on Mars were similar to Earth.

Sketch made by William Herschel in 1777

As the astronomers kept on pointing out more and more things about Mars, it became apparent that the Red Planet is the most Earth-like of all the planets in the solar system. To them, the surface features on Mars looked like the planet had land and seas just like Earth. A day on Mars was nearly as long as one on Earth. Mars was tilted a little more than Earth and it had seasons like Earth. Mars had white polar caps like Earth. With all these similarities, Mars did not appear to be all that different from Earth. So, when the nineteenth century dawned, people seriously thought that there could be life on Mars.

Maps of Mars

Telescopes had become very sophisticated by the middle of the nineteenth century. Astronomers who peered at Mars through these telescopes found more and more fascinating facets of the Red Planet. They also prepared detailed maps of the surface features of Mars from drawings based on their observations of the planet.

The astronomers who created maps of Mars were called aerographers, and the new field of study they had started was called aerography. It was named after Ares, the Greek god of war.

Aerography involved following several steps in preparing a map of a planet. First, the aerographer had to make factual drawings of the features of the planet that had been observed through the telescope. Then, a note had to be appended, describing the clarity of seeing the planet, precise colouring and shading, contrast and so on. When the aerographer completed his observation, he was required to produce a high quality colour drawing under good light conditions, based on the sketches made and notes taken at the time of viewing the planet through the telescope.

During the first half of the nineteenth century, it came to be accepted that the light areas seen on Mars were continents and the dark areas were seas. It also became commonplace to name these surface features, and while doing so, the names of the astronomers who had identified these features first, were preferred. That is how we came to have Cassini land, Herschel Straight and Maraldi Sea.

The mysterious canals on Mars

In 1877, there was a perihelic opposition and it brought Mars as close as 57 million kilometres to Earth. This was a wonderful opportunity for astronomers to study Mars even more closely. Giovanni Schiaparelli, an Italian astronomer, had already acquired a reputation for being an excellent observer of planets, and more importantly, he now had his 8.6-inch refracting telescope to watch Mars during the time of its perihelic opposition.

Schiaparelli trained his telescope on Mars, and was amazed to see some features on the surface no other astronomer had seen before. There were straight, narrow lines connecting larger dark areas with each other. So great was his amazement at this startling discovery that he promptly settled down to devise a 62-point reference system on the globe of Mars by which he could precisely chart the position of these straight lines.

As was the practice those days, Schiaparelli gave them a name. He called them 'canali', an Italian word that translates into channel in English. But due to some confusion, it was accepted in English as 'canal'. The confusion had something to do with the Suez Canal which had just been completed, and everyone was talking about this great technical and engineering feat. Canals were in fashion and that was how Schiaparelli's discovery was accepted in English.

Soon, word got around that Schiaparelli had seen canals on the surface of Mars. This caused great excitement but when other astronomers looked through their telescopes to see Schiaparelli's canals on Mars, they could not see any. Some astronomers openly expressed their doubts about the existence of these straight lines on the surface of Mars.

Schiaparelli was a determined man. He now sat down and devised a more elaborate 114-point reference system and invented new methods of contrasting the features on Mars. During the next opposition of Mars, which occurred in 1879, he used his new system while observing Mars. He now came out with the claim that he could see more canals and more clearly.

During the opposition of Mars that occurred in 1881, Schiaparelli looked at Mars even more diligently and used his elaborate reference system. This time, he claimed that he could clearly see twenty canals. He also claimed that he could see these canals splitting into two. Where he had previously observed only a single straight line, he could now clearly see two in the place of one.

Other astronomers struggled in vain to see

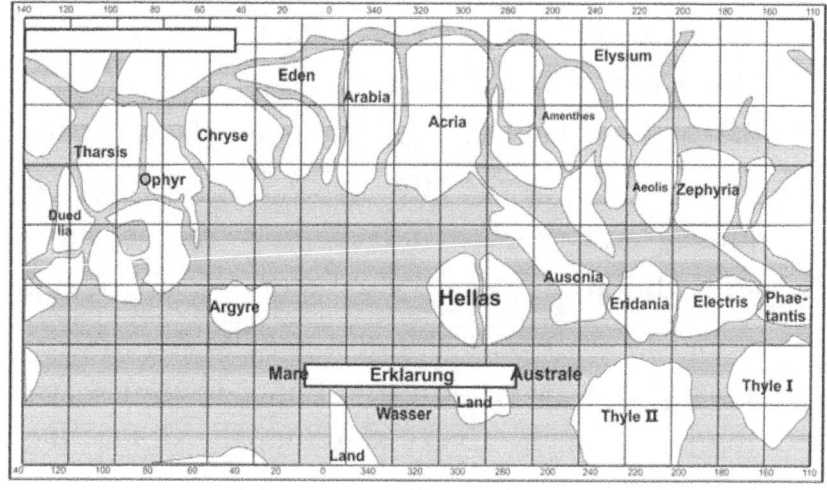

Schiaparelli's Canals

these straight lines on the surface of Mars. Schiaparelli pointed out that it was not easy to see these lines. That was because one could see them only at exceptional times, and that too, for fleeting moments. Schiaparelli spoke so convincingly about these canals on Mars that the subject evoked considerable interest around the world. It caused a lot of speculation, too. Colourful stories began to be told of how Schiaparelli had seen canals on Mars, which were built by a race of intelligent Martians.

Schiaparelli's canals gained credibility in

the mid-1880s when two major observatories confirmed sighting these canals precisely where Schiaparelli had said he had seen them. These observatories were the Nice Observatory in France and the Lick Observatory in the USA. In addition, the Lick Observatory reported that they had seen several bright patches on Mars in the region between day and night. The press put the news out in a very sensational manner: the Martians were signalling to Earth using giant flashing lights. Schiaparelli's canals had really excited the public imagination.

It is at this point that Percival Lowell appeared on the scene. He came from a rich American family that owned a lucrative business in textiles. Lowell was not at all interested in the family business. He had developed a passion for the Red Planet. He had read a popular book on Mars that had got him interested in the planet. Schiaparelli's canals caught his fancy and he was convinced that these canals did exist. He decided to build an observatory and see these canals for himself.

From his observatory in Arizona, Lowell

had a good look at Mars and thought he saw Schiaparelli's canals. Now he proposed a very romantic theory. He suggested that during the summer months in the southern hemisphere in Mars, the polar ice cap would partially melt and provide running water to the rest of the planet through an intricate network of canals built by an ancient, intelligent and technologically advanced race of Martians.

Lowell even calculated the length of these canals and the rate of flow of water in them. He suggested that some of the canals were over 2,000 kilometres long, and that water flowed through them at the rate of 3 kilometres per hour. As the summer on Mars progressed, the canals filled up, and the vegetation on either side of the canals was watered, and the vegetation blossomed, making it visible to people on Earth.

Lowell's conclusions were flashed in newspapers all across the United States. He also travelled widely and lectured to audiences about his findings. Schiaparelli continued his observations of Mars and kept confirming the existence of canals. As a result, people came to accept that the canals on Mars were real. Added to this, Lowell's conclusions about these canals being built by an advanced race of Martians fired the popular imagination.

It was only when Mariner 4, the first space probe to successfully reach Mars, sent back pictures of the planet in July 1965 that there was an end to the controversy about canals. From the pictures it was clear that there was neither any canal nor any sign of life on Mars. It was a completely dead planet.

Mars in the imagination

The theory that Mars was home to an intelligent race of living beings made it a hot subject for science fiction writers. One of the best science fiction books about Mars was *Two Planets* written by Kurd Lasswitz in 1897. Lasswitz described Martians as a race much older, more advanced and intelligent than ours.

Originally written in German, the book became

a classic in German-speaking countries. It was later translated into English.

Edgar Rice Burroughs wrote a number of books about Mars in the early years of the twentieth century. These books came out in a series called the Mars series and were hugely popular. In these books, Burroughs wrote about the struggle of one John Carter with creatures in a land high up in the sky, which was full of dry deserts.

H.G. Wells, considered to be the father of science fiction, wrote the popular story about Mars, *War of the Worlds*. This story was originally published in serial form in *Cosmopolitan* magazine in 1897, and came out as a book the next year. It begins with astronomers observing strange flashes on Mars, and before they come to know anything, a band of nasty Martians invade the British isles causing a lot of destruction and devastation.

War of the Worlds became very popular, a large part of it due to Orson Welles, the famous movie producer. Welles produced a radio play about Martians attacking the United States. The play carried fabricated news reports about the Martian attack. It also carried interviews with eyewitnesses, which were all fabricated. When the radio play was aired, it created panic throughout the United States. Americans thought that Martians had really attacked their country.

Another famous book about Mars is Ray Bradbury's *The Martian Chronicles*. The book talks of Mars as a place where people can live without any technical aids. The air is thin, the wind is dry and the conditions are more or less similar to those in Earth's deserts.

Arthur C. Clarke's novel *The Sands of Mars* came a year after Ray Bradbury's book. In Clarke's novel, Mars had been conquered, and was inhabited by kangaroo-like animals, adapted to the dry climate but with intelligence close to that of dogs.

These are among the more famous science fiction books written during that period, but there were many more. These fictional books imagined that there was life on Mars, and the Red Planet was very much like our planet Earth. These writers told stories of people travelling to

Mars through supernatural methods, or through the use of some alien technology. An exception to this was the novel *Daybreak: A Romance of an Old World* by James Cowan, in which humans reached Mars through a fluke of astronomy. In Cowan's story, the Moon entered Earth's atmosphere and settled into the Pacific Ocean. While an expedition was exploring the Moon, it broke loose and transported the members of the expedition to Mars.

The stories that these books told were visionary. They made it seem that almost anything was possible. They may sound absurd in the light of what we know about the planet Mars now, but they achieved something very important. These stories inspired a generation of space scientists and rocket pioneers. Wernher von Braun, a rocket pioneer, often mentioned that just as American space scientists had been influenced by a childhood fascination with Burroughs' Martian novels, many German rocket scientists had, as children, buried themselves in the pages of *Two Planets*.

3

Missions to Mars

Studying Mars through a telescope has its limits. Even with the largest telescope, it is almost impossible to see the small but important details on Mars. With a telescope all one can see are the big things on it like the polar caps and albedo features. (Albedo features are those big features that can be seen in the light reflected by the surface of the planet.) It is only with the beginning of the space age that it became possible to see and analyse the Red Planet in detail.

The Space Age

The Space Age began when the then Soviet Union launched Sputnik 1, the world's first satellite. The rocket with Sputnik 1 blasted off on 4 October 1957. Though it was a small satellite and took only 98 minutes to orbit Earth, its successful launch was a historic event. Humanity had won over the force of gravity. It was a great triumph for science and technology.

A month later, the Soviet Union launched its second satellite that was heavier than Sputnik 1. It had an animal on board. Sputnik 3 was launched on 15 May 1958. It carried a number of research instruments.

With these satellites travelling in space, it became possible to approach the planets. A satellite could now observe planets from close quarters. These satellites, which explore space, are not satellites in the strict sense of the term. A satellite is something that orbits another body. The satellites going into space are actually space probes that travel deep into the solar system. On their journeys, they send back detailed pictures and other data of faraway planets and other celestial bodies. These are called spacecraft, but in their design and functions, they are very similar to orbiting satellites.

Spacecraft can be of three kinds: a fly-by mission, an orbiter or a lander. A fly-by spacecraft travels on a path at a distance from the planet and while flying by, makes observations of the planet and takes photographs. An orbiting spacecraft goes in an orbit around the planet and the instruments in the spacecraft make observations and take photographs. A lander is first put in an orbit around the planet and then commanded to land on the surface. A rover then comes out and travels over the surface of the planet to make scientific observations.

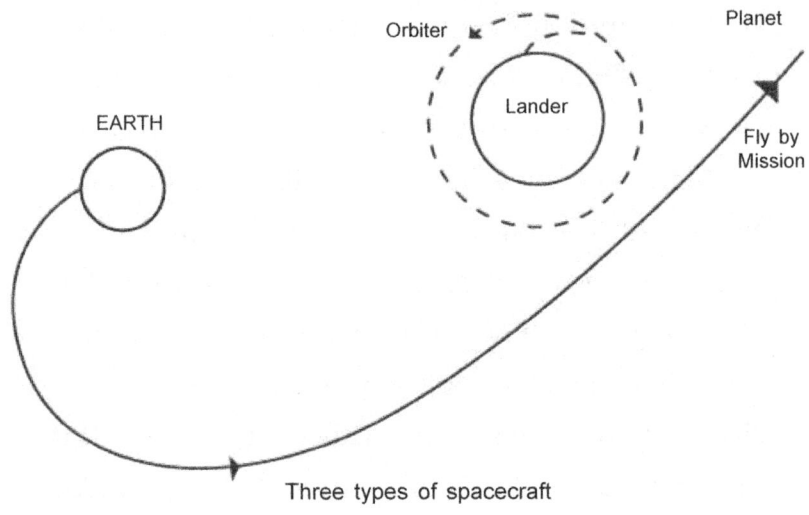

Three types of spacecraft

Mars missions by Soviet Union/Russia

It was soon after the Soviet Union sent Sputnik 1 and 2 to space that it started thinking of sending probes to Mars. The first Mars project, Project 1M, began in 1959. The project proposed two fly-by spacecraft to be sent to Mars to obtain images of the Martian surface. The spacecraft carried several instruments including photo-television cameras to take pictures and transmitters to transfer pictures to Earth. Both the spacecraft were launched in October 1960, but the rockets carrying the spacecraft crashed and neither spacecraft could enter the flight trajectory to Mars.

In the spring of 1961, work was started on Project 2MV. The idea was to explore Mars with a fly-by spacecraft as well as with a lander. The spacecraft Mars 1 was launched on 1 November 1962. The launch was successful and the spacecraft travelled on the trajectory to Mars. But the information transmitted by the spacecraft was of no use. Finally, after five months, the transmitters on the spacecraft fell silent. The last radio contact was when the spacecraft was 106 million kilometres from Earth.

The Soviet Union subsequently planned five more missions to Mars from 1964 to 1971. Most of them failed for various reasons. These were Zond 1 and Zond 2 in 1964. While the launch of Zond 1 did not succeed, Zond 2 was put in an inter-planetary trajectory but could not fulfil its mission because the solar panels of the spacecraft did not open. In 1969, there were two identical missions, M-69A and M-69B. M-69A spacecraft took off smoothly but an explosion in the third stage of the rocket shortly after lift-off finished the flight. M-69B too failed when after the rocket lifted off, a steam of black smoke appeared in the right engine. A few seconds later there was a loud explosion and the

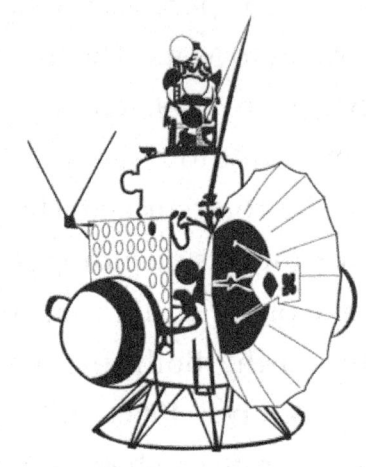

Mars 1 spacecraft

rocket became a huge ball of fire.

In 1971, Earth and Mars were at a minimum distance from each other. That happens once in fifteen to seventeen years and it is a good time for observing Mars. It is also the time when a spacecraft requires less power to travel to Mars and therefore it is possible to launch a heavier spacecraft. So the Soviet Union decided to send a heavy probe, M-71, to Mars. M-71 was designed as an orbiter and was launched on 5 May 1971. The spacecraft started orbiting Earth and was ready for being put on the trajectory to Mars but due to a wrong command issued by an operator, the mission failed.

The next two probes—Mars 2 and Mars 3—carried both orbiters and landers. The Mars 2 launch was successful and it reached Mars in November 1971. On 27 November 1971 the lander of Mars 2 crash-landed on the surface of Mars because an onboard computer malfunctioned. But it became the first man-made object to touch down on Mars.

Mars 3 was launched two days after Mars 2. It

was a successful launch and on 2 December 1971 its lander touched down on Mars as planned. It became the first spacecraft to attain a soft landing on Mars. But transmission from the lander was interrupted after 14.6 seconds, and so no useful data could be sent by the lander to Earth.

However, the orbiters of Mars 2 and Mars 3 worked well and they sent back a large volume of data about the temperature and atmospheric pressure on the Martian surface and the nature of rocks. These orbiters sent colourful images of the surface of Mars to Earth.

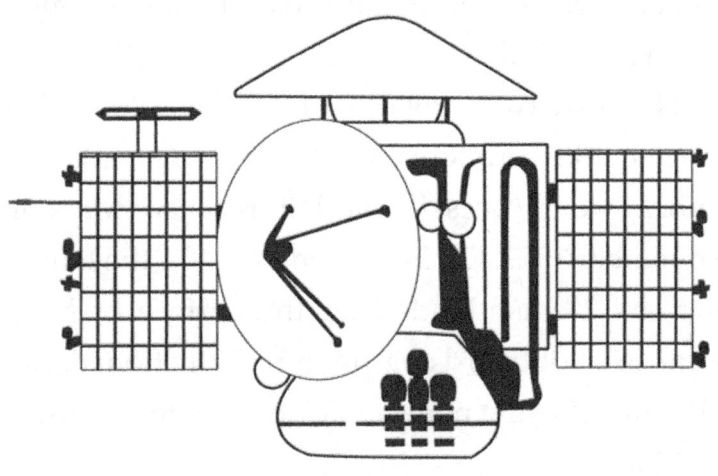

Mars 3 spacecraft

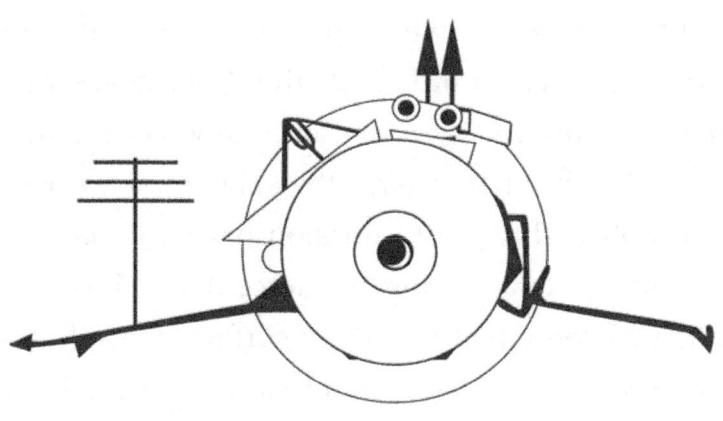

Mars 3 spacecraft

In 1973, the Soviet Union sent four more probes to Mars. They were Mars 4 and 5 (both orbiters), and Mars 6 and Mars 7 (fly-by and lander combinations). Mars 4 and 5 spacecraft were launched earlier so that they could arrive in time to receive the data from Mars 6 and 7 landers.

All the missions except Mars 7 sent back data to Earth. Mars 7 went to the wrong orbit. Mars 4 came within 2,200 kilometres of Mars' orbit and took images of Mars from its fly-by trajectory and sent them to Earth. But the spacecraft did not enter Mars' orbit.

Mars 6 stopped sending information two

months after it was launched. During the remaining five months of its flight, the spacecraft operated on its own without any commands from Earth. However, the silent spacecraft accomplished its flight mission partly. Its lander sent some data during its descent to Mars but failed as soon as it hit Mars' surface. Only Mars 5 spacecraft completed its mission successfully. It went into Mars' orbit and sent back sixty images of the planet to Earth.

The Soviet Union sent two more probes in 1989 — Phobos 1 and Phobos 2 — to study Mars and its two moons. The first spacecraft lost contact with Earth while on its way to Mars. The second spacecraft took photographs of Mars and Phobos but failed before it could release its two landers to land on the surface of Phobos.

In 1996, the Russian Government planned the Mars 96 spacecraft mission to study the planet from its orbit with penetrators dropped to the Martian surface. The mission failed because the spacecraft was not injected in the inter-planetary trajectory.

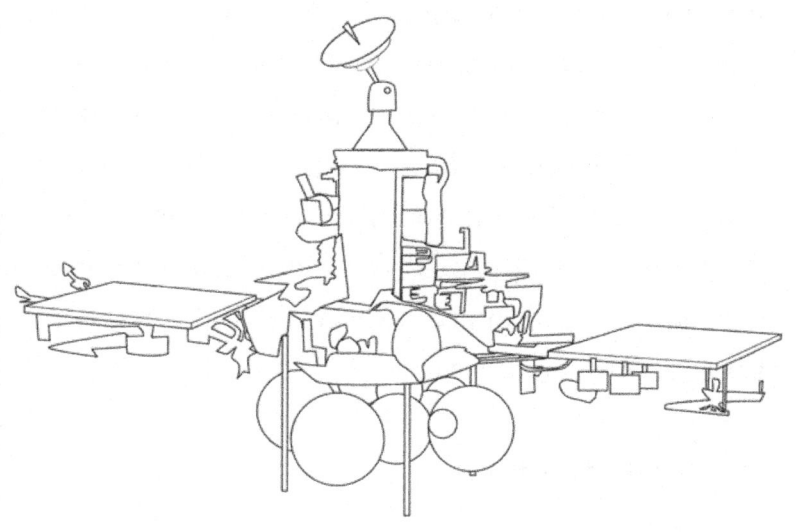

Phobos 2 spacecraft

In 2011, the Fobos-Grunt lander spacecraft, which was to land on Phobos and return samples, was launched. But it failed to leave Earth's orbit and fell back to Earth.

The US Missions

When the Soviet Union launched Sputnik 1, the immediate effect of the launch was to startle the American public and create a sense of panic that the Soviet Union had got the better of the United States. In a bid to restore confidence at home and prestige abroad, the American government took several measures in the area of space. One of them was to start the National Aeronautics and Space Administration (NASA) for the advancement of aeronautics and space science. NASA then sent several missions to Mars.

Mariner Programme

In 1964, NASA planned two missions to Mars, Mariner 3 and Mariner 4. These two missions were fly-by spacecraft. Mariner 3 was a failure, but Mariner 4 was a success. The spacecraft took seven and half months to reach Mars. On 15 July 1965, it took twenty-one black and white pictures of the southern hemisphere of Mars as it flew at a distance of 9,600 kilometres from the planet. These pictures showed Mars to be a world of craters, almost like the Moon, and there was no sign of surface water on Mars. Mariner 4 found no sign of Martian life either.

NASA continued the Mariner programme with another pair of fly-by probes — Mariner 6 and 7. Mariner 6 took seventy-four images of the southern hemisphere that showed it was a forbidding landscape marked by craters.

Mariner 7 flew over the southern hemisphere of Mars and took 126 images of the Hellas basin with its smooth floor, Hellespontus region with its craters and the ice cap at the south pole. The images taken by Mariner 6 and Mariner 7 showed Mars to be a dry and desert landscape of sand rocks.

Mariner 8 and 9 spacecrafts were designed as orbiters. Mariner 8 failed at launch. Mariner 9 was successful and started orbiting Mars in November 1971. At that time, a huge dust storm was raging across Mars, and Mariner 9 could not take any clear picture because the entire planet was covered with dust and nothing could be seen of the surface. Mariner 9 was reprogrammed to wait for the dust storm to disperse.

The storm subsided only in December, and Mariner 9 took several pictures of the planet. The pictures showed Mars to be two-faced. One face was the northern hemisphere with its smooth, low lands. The southern hemisphere had highlands and craters. Mariner 9 also found some evidence that liquid water might have flowed on the Martian surface at one time. The pictures taken by Mariner 9 showed channels tens of kilometres wide. These channels started in the highlands of the southern hemisphere and opened out into the smooth plains of the northern hemisphere. Mariner 9 sent more than 7,200 photographs to Earth.

Viking Mission

The Viking mission consisted of two spacecraft— Viking 1 and Viking 2. Each spacecraft had a lander powered by nuclear energy and an orbiter powered by energy from the Sun. Viking 1 arrived at Mars in June 1976. Viking 2 reached Mars in August 1976. These two were the first spacecraft landers to successfully land on Mars.

Both the Viking landers and orbiters had long

lives. Viking 1 orbiter functioned till August 1980. Together with the Viking 2 orbiter, it returned more than 51,500 images, mapping 97 per cent of the Martian surface, Though the Viking 1 lander was supposed to function only for ninety days, it sent back data for more than six years.

The images sent by the Viking mission showed hundreds of branching channels on Mars, most of them the size of a river. This was in addition to the large channels seen by the Mariner 9 spacecraft. Most of these channels were in the southern hemisphere. These channels seemed to indicate a point of time in the distant past when the planet had a dense, warm atmosphere.

The Viking mission was a huge success in terms of what it found on Mars. But it had been designed as a mission for finding life on Mars. Unfortunately, the results of the biological experiments conducted by the Viking landers did not offer any final proof. The Viking 1 lander scooped dirt from the top few centimetres of the Martian surface and carried out tests. Later, both Viking 1 and Viking 2 landers scooped additional samples, even pushing aside rocks to sample underneath the Martian surface, and repeated the tests. But the results were not clear.

The Viking probes may not have found final evidence of life on Mars, but the pictures they took showed the dusty red surface of the planet covered with red rocks under a pink sky. At last we came to know what it was like on Mars.

Mars Global Surveyor

Mars Global Surveyor, an orbiter, was launched in November 1997 and entered Mars' orbit in September 1998 after a ten-month flight. It took about a year and half to trim its elliptical orbit and come to a circular orbit around the planet. It began mapping Mars in March 1999 and continued for one Martian year (equivalent of two Earth years).

Mars Global Surveyor studied the entire Martian surface, atmosphere and interior of the planet. It sent back more information about Mars than all the previous Mars missions combined. It took pictures of the gullies and debris flow. These

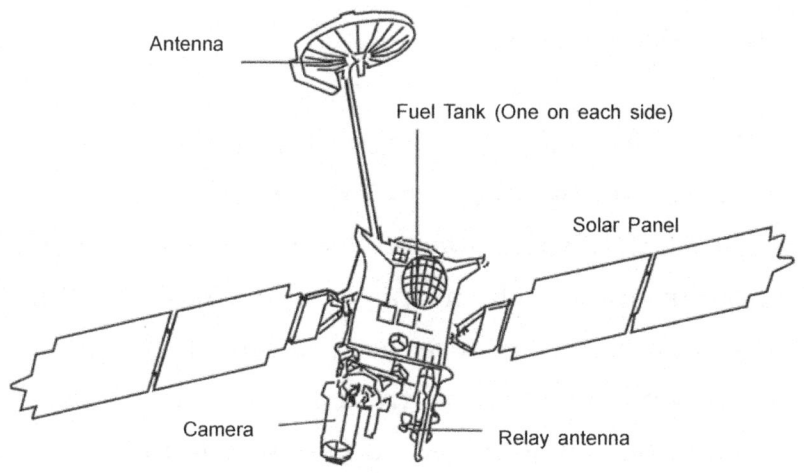

Mars Global Surveyor

pictures suggested that there may be current sources of liquid water at or near the surface of the planet.

Mars Pathfinder

Mars Pathfinder spacecraft successfully landed on Mars in July 1997. It consisted of a lander and a robotic rover. It was a successful mission, which validated technologies like airbag landing system and automated obstacle avoidance system. We will talk about this mission in greater detail in the next chapter.

Mars Polar Lander

Mars Polar Lander spacecraft was designed to land in the southern polar area of Mars. The spacecraft also contained Deep Space 2 (DS2), a mini-probe, which was supposed to hit the Martian polar surface at a diminished speed and send information from below the ground. Mars Polar Lander was successfully launched in January 1999 and was expected to land on the Martian polar surface in December 1999. But it was destroyed while attempting a landing. The retro-rockets were shut off when the probe was still at an altitude of dozens of metres from the Martian surface, and it fell like a rock on the ground. DS2, the mini-probe, was also lost in the process.

Mars Odyssey

Mars Odyssey, an orbiter, reached Mars in October 2001. Its mission was to use spectrometers and imagers to look for evidence of past or present water and volcanic activity. With its spectrometers, Odyssey found that much of the Martian ground is loaded with ice. In 2002, its spectrometers detected large amounts of hydrogen. This was an important discovery because it means that we may find vast deposits of water ice in the upper three metres of Mars' soil in the southern polar region.

Mars Exploration Rover

The Mars Exploration Rover mission consisted of two rovers — Spirit and Opportunity — that would look for signs of water in the terrain, soil and rocks. The idea was to find geological clues whether parts of Mars formerly had environments wet enough to be hospitable to life. Both reached Mars in January 2004. While Spirit stopped working in 2009, Opportunity is still roving the surface of Mars. Both the missions of Mars Exploration Rover programme were very successful.

Mars Reconnaissance Orbiter

Mars Reconnaissance Orbiter was designed to conduct reconnaissance and exploration of Mars from the orbit. The spacecraft reached Mars' orbit in March 2006. It is currently operational and its scientific instruments are being used to analyse Martian landforms and detect water, ice and minerals on and below the surface. It also monitors the weather and surface conditions on Mars, searches for landing sites and is testing a new communication system to send and receive information to and from Earth faster and more efficiently.

Mars Science Laboratory

Mars Science Laboratory along with its rover Curiosity landed on Mars on 6 August 2012. The rover is carrying instruments to look for past or present conditions that were or are suitable for making Mars habitable. The mission is operational.

European Space Agency missions

Mars Express Orbiter

Mars Express Orbiter with its lander Beagle 2 reached Mars' orbit on 25 December 2003 and Beagle 2 entered the atmosphere of Mars on the same day. However, attempts to contact Beagle 2 failed and the lander was declared to be lost.

Mars Express Orbiter carries an instrument called MARSIS to find out how much frozen water is there in the ice sheets in the polar region of Mars. Mars Express has confirmed the presence of water ice and carbon dioxide at the south pole of the planet. The mission is still operational.

Japanese Probe

Japan launched the Nozomi (Planet-B) probe to Mars in July 1998. It was an orbiter. Unfortunately, the spacecraft used up too much fuel during a trajectory correction manoeuvre and could not reach Mars' orbit. After years of trying to retrieve the spacecraft, the mission was finally terminated in December 2003.

Chinese Probe

The Chinese launched their first Mars probe, Yinghuo 1, on 8 November 2011. But the probe was stranded in space and a week after the launch China declared that the probe was lost.

In the last five decades, as many as forty-two Mars probes have been attempted. Of them, twenty-two probes have been failures. If the successes of the past twelve years were to be omitted, the number of successes would be cut down to half. In spite of the numerous failures, the technical and scientific achievements of the Mars exploration effort during this period have been invaluable.

Why have there been so many failures? The main reason is that in the early years of Mars probes, every facet of each mission to Mars had to be conceived, invented, tried and tested from scratch. There was no precedent. It was all new and risky. In addition, the complexity and length of the missions to Mars made it likely that failures could occur.

The failure rate is so high that the missions launched from Earth to study Mars are called the Martian Curse. Donald Neff, a journalist with Time magazine coined the phrase 'Great Galactic Ghoul' to describe the fictitious space monster who devours these missions to Mars. The Great Galactic Ghoul lives in the area between Earth and Mars, and the ghoul's staple diet is the planetary probes sent by poor uninformed humans!

4

The Robotic Rover

Robots have been our scouts on Mars, acting as our eyes and ears on the planet. Some robots observe the planet from a distance while others land there, roving on the Martian surface and gathering samples for close inspection and analysis. Since robots are machines, they have fewer needs and can endure hostile conditions better than humans.

The first few missions flew near Mars and took pictures of the planet from a distance. The pictures revealed to us a planet that looks like our Moon. There are large and small craters spread over the surface. Subsequent pictures showed us Olympus Mons, the largest known volcano in the solar system. The robots gave us insights into the different regions of the planet: the southern part that was older, consisting of highlands which are full of craters; and the northern part which is younger, consisting of volcanic plains and lowlands, and channels that looked like ancient riverbeds.

The next few missions both orbited and landed on Mars. In addition to taking photographs and collecting data, the landers carried out scientific experiments. Some of these experiments looked for signs of life on Mars. The robots helped scientists to map and analyse the surface of Mars, and explore its atmosphere, surface and sub-surface. The next generation of robots is being designed to identify sites for human settlement on Mars and look for resources that will enable humans to live on the planet.

Robotic Rover

A rover is a kind of mobile robotic spacecraft that scientists can send to the surface of a planet and control remotely from Earth. Rovers are useful when scientists want to explore places that humans cannot visit or have not visited or when the conditions on the planet make human exploration difficult. So far, the Moon and Mars are the only two places beyond Earth, which have been visited by rovers.

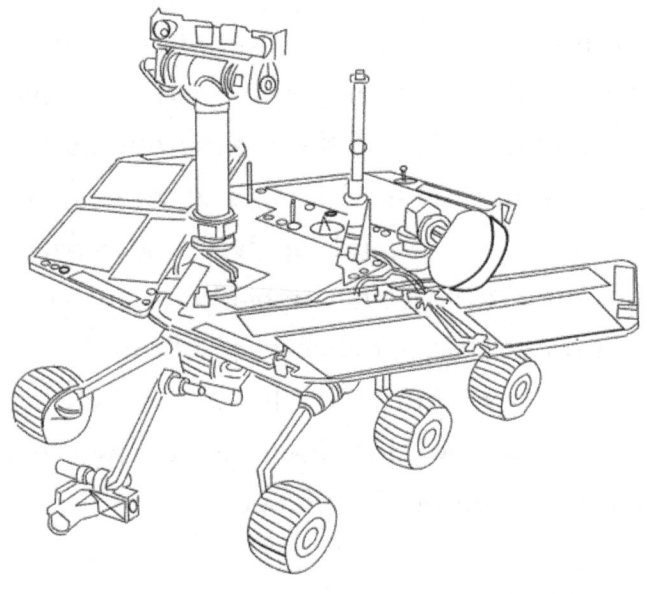

Robotic rover

In a rover mission, the robotic rover and the instruments it carries are the centrepieces of the mission. But the success of the rover mission depends on the performance of other elements of the mission: launch vehicle, cruise stage, system for entering Mars' atmosphere, descending through it and landing, the lander, and system for communicating with the team controlling it from Earth.

These rovers function as robotic field geologists. They examine sites on the planet for clues about what has happened there. The clues are in the rocks but it is difficult to go to every rock. So, a panoramic camera at human eye height and a miniature thermal emission spectrometer which measures the amount of heat coming from the surface help scientists identify the most interesting rocks likely to provide them with clues.

It is to these rocks that the rovers go. The rover can watch for hazards as it roves and avoid them. The rover is mounted on six wheels and its power comes from an array of solar panels each the size of a dining table. The rover drives to the selected rock and extends an arm that has

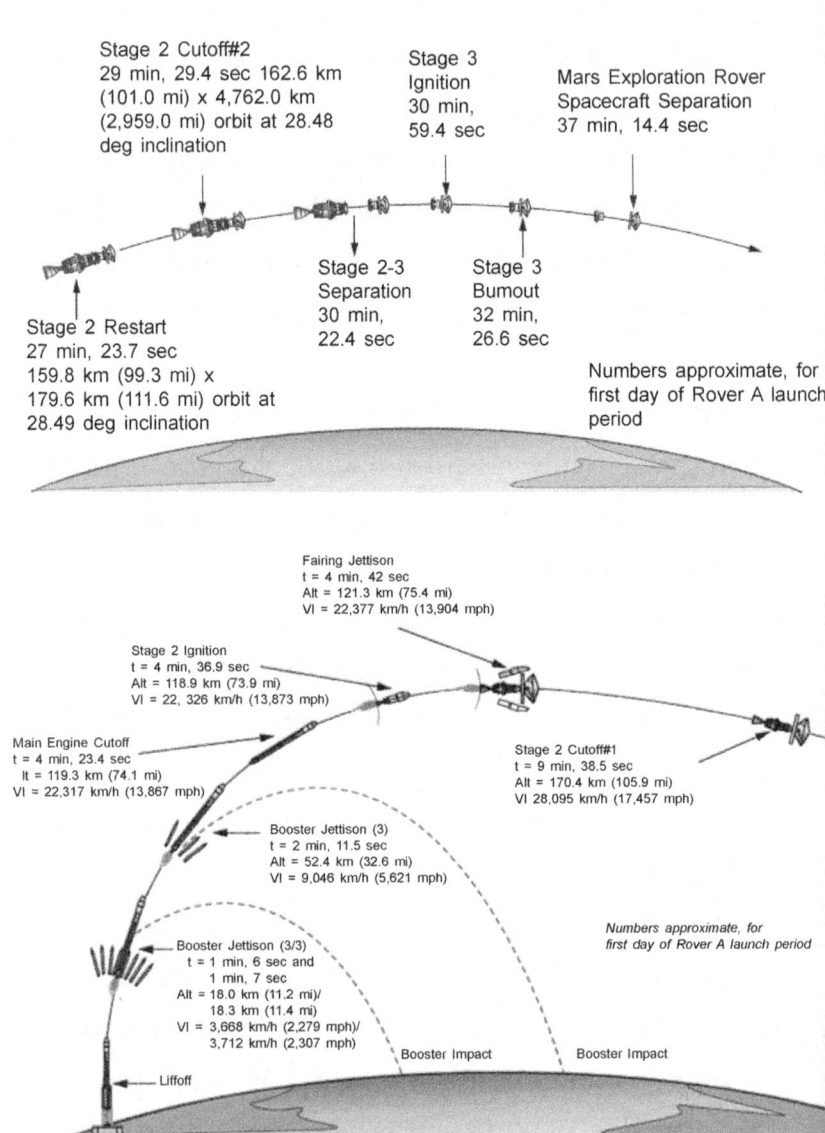

Stage 2 Cutoff#2
29 min, 29.4 sec 162.6 km
(101.0 mi) x 4,762.0 km
(2,959.0 mi) orbit at 28.48
deg inclination

Stage 3
Ignition
30 min,
59.4 sec

Mars Exploration Rover
Spacecraft Separation
37 min, 14.4 sec

Stage 2-3
Separation
30 min,
22.4 sec

Stage 3
Bumout
32 min,
26.6 sec

Stage 2 Restart
27 min, 23.7 sec
159.8 km (99.3 mi) x
179.6 km (111.6 mi) orbit at
28.49 deg inclination

Numbers approximate, for
first day of Rover A launch
period

Fairing Jettison
t = 4 min, 42 sec
Alt = 121.3 km (75.4 mi)
VI = 22,377 km/h (13,904 mph)

Stage 2 Ignition
t = 4 min, 36.9 sec
Alt = 118.9 km (73.9 mi)
VI = 22, 326 km/h (13,873 mph)

Main Engine Cutoff
t = 4 min, 23.4 sec
lt = 119.3 km (74.1 mi)
VI = 22,317 km/h (13,867 mph)

A

Stage 2 Cutoff#1
t = 9 min, 38.5 sec
Alt = 170.4 km (105.9 mi)
VI 28,095 km/h (17,457 mph)

Booster Jettison (3)
t = 2 min, 11.5 sec
Alt = 52.4 km (32.6 mi)
VI = 9,046 km/h (5,621 mph)

Numbers approximate, for
first day of Rover A launch period

Booster Jettison (3/3)
t = 1 min, 6 sec and
1 min, 7 sec
Alt = 18.0 km (11.2 mi)/
18.3 km (11.4 mi)
VI = 3,668 km/h (2,279 mph)/
3,712 km/h (2,307 mph)

Booster Impact

Booster Impact

Liffoff

Launch phases

tools at the end of it. Then, a microscopic imager, just like the lens a geologist holds in his hand gives a close-up view of the texture of the rock. Two spectrometers identify the composition of the rock. The fourth tool on the rover is like the geologist's hammer. It exposes the interior of the rock by scraping away the weathered surface.

The size of the rover varies. For example, Sojourner, the rover in the Pathfinder mission, was tiny: it was 2 feet long and weighed 10 kg. Spirit and Opportunity, the rovers of the Mars Exploration Rover mission, were 4.9 feet long and weighed 174 kg. Curiosity, the rover of the Mars Science Laboratory mission, is 9.5 feet long and weighs 899 kg.

In the rover, the core structure is made of composite honeycomb material. The core body, called the warm electronics box, is topped with a triangular surface called the rover equipment deck. The deck has three antennas, a camera mast and a panel of solar cells.

Each rover is equipped with a six-wheel drive. It has a suspension system that bends at its joints;

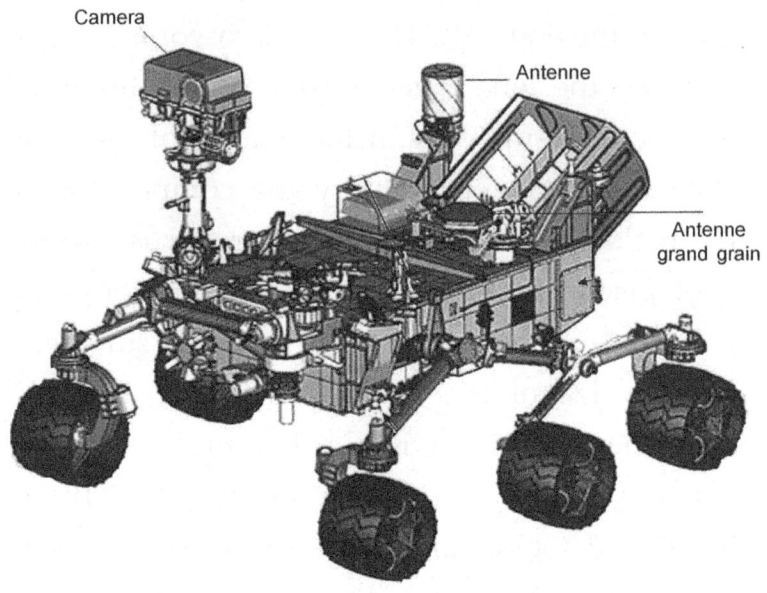

Camera

Antenne

Antenne
grand grain

Parts of the robotic rover

it does not use springs. The joints allow the rover to roll over rocks that are bigger than the diameter of its wheels. For example, Spirit and Opportunity have wheels with a diameter of 10 inches but in the case of Curiosity, the diameter of the wheels is 20 inches.

The Spirit and Opportunity rovers can withstand a tilt of 45 degrees in any direction without overturning. In the case of Curiosity, the tilt tolerated is of 50 degrees. The rovers have independent steering of front and rear wheels, which allows them to turn or drive in gradual arcs. Each wheel has a pattern that leaves patterned tracks in the sandy surface of Mars. This pattern helps the on-board cameras to judge the distance travelled by the rover.

The rover is fitted with navigation software, which gives it hazard-avoiding capabilities that it can use to make its way towards a destination. Two stereo pairs of hazard identification cameras are mounted below the deck of the rover, one at the front of the rover and the other at the rear. Curiosity can roll over obstacles of about 26 inches in height and it has a ground clearance of 24 inches. It can travel up to 295 feet per hour but the average speed is about one-third of that.

There are two powerful on-board computers on the rover. These computers contain radiation-hardened memory to tolerate the extreme radiation from space and to safeguard against power-off cycles.

The science instruments of the rover are kept at the end of the robotic arm, called the Instrument

Deployment Device. This is tucked away under the front of the rover while it is travelling. The robotic arm extends forward when the rover wants to examine a particular rock or patch of soil.

The rovers are equipped with communication systems through which they can talk to the science team on Earth either directly or through the orbiter. For example, Curiosity can communicate directly with Earth, but the bulk of the data transfer is relayed through the two orbiters Mars Reconnaissance Orbiter and Mars Odyssey orbiter. Signals require an average of 14 minutes and 6 seconds to travel between Mars and Earth.

Lander

The lander provides the platform from which the rover can roll on to the Martian surface. The sides of the lander open like petals. The lander's basic structure consists of four triangular petals made of composite material. Three petals are attached with a hinge to an edge of the central base petal. The rover stays fastened to the base petal during

A view of a lander

the flight of the spacecraft and landing. When folded up, the petals of the lander form a box in which the rover is kept safely.

Launch Vehicle

The launch vehicle that carries the lander and the rover is usually a high-powered rocket. For example, the launch vehicle in the case of missions like Pathfinder and Mars Exploration Rovers (Spirit and Opportunity) was a Delta II rocket. This rocket has a history of more than 40 successful launches.

Launch vehicles, which carry spacecraft, have stages. In case of staging, a big rocket is put at the bottom, a smaller one on top of it, a still smaller rocket on top of the second one, another rocket on the third one, and then, the satellite on top of the fourth rocket. In flight, when the big rocket (the first stage) is empty, it falls away. The second rocket (second stage) fires and carries the third and fourth stages with the satellite to higher altitudes. When the third stage is empty, the fourth stage does its job by carrying the satellite to the necessary height. Strap-on boosters are the additional rocket boosters that provide extra energy to the launch vehicle and thereby increase the capability of the vehicle. Strap-on boosters are commonly used in most rockets. Fairing is the place on top of the launch vehicle where the satellite is kept. When the launch vehicle reaches its destination, the fairing opens, releasing the satellite.

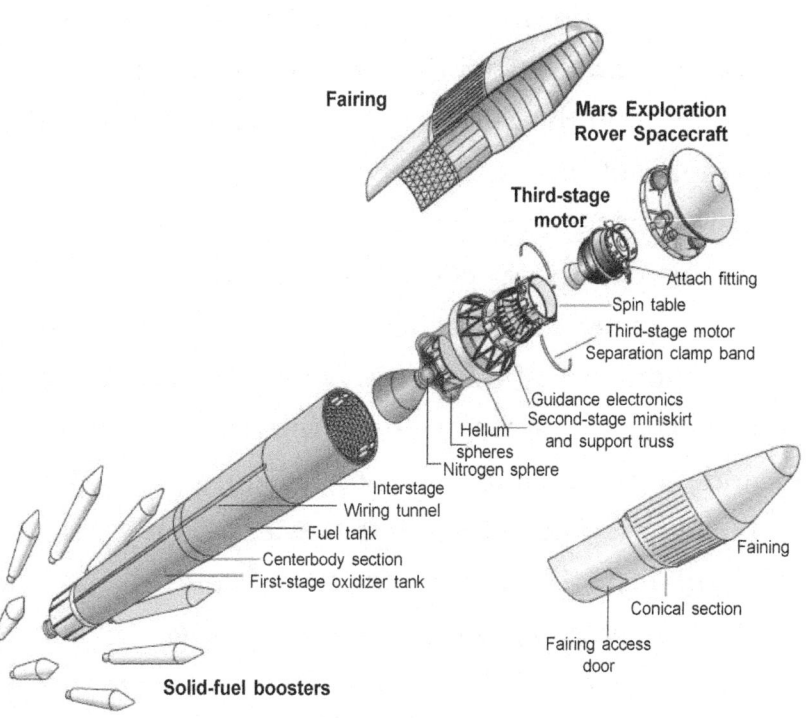

Delta II Rocket

Delta II is a three-stage vehicle. When it is launched, its first-stage engine and six of its nine strap-on boosters ignite the moment the rocket lifts off. The remaining three boosters ignite following burnout of the first six. After 4 minutes and 23 seconds into the flight, the main engine is cut off. Within the following 20 seconds, the first stage separates from the second, the second stage ignites, and the fairing falls away. After about 10 minutes of lift-off, the second stage engine stops firing temporarily.

At this point, the spacecraft with the second and third stages still attached to it, is in an orbit of 167 kilometres above Earth. Before it can complete one orbit, the second stage of the rocket re-ignites and starts pushing the rocket into the inter-planetary trajectory towards Mars. This begins about 14 to 19 minutes after the lift-off

At this time, small rockets are fired to start the engine of the third stage. The third stage then separates from the second, and fires its engine for about 87 seconds to finish putting the spacecraft on the course to Mars. The spacecraft now sheds the burnt-out third stage. It happens about 34 to 39 minutes after the lift-off. Springs push the third stage away, exposing an antenna on the rover spacecraft's cruise stage.

Cruise stage

The journey to Mars takes about seven months. The first phase of the journey is called the cruise phase. The final fifteen days before arrival on Mars are known as the approach phase. During both these phases, the spacecraft is attached to the cruise stage that will be jettisoned in the final few minutes of the flight.

The rover spacecraft looks like a nested set of Russian dolls. The rover travels to Mars tucked inside the folded-up lander wrapped in airbags. The lander, in turn, is encased in a protective aeroshell. Finally, the disc-shaped cruise stage is attached to the aeroshell on one side and to the launch vehicle on the other.

Mars has an atmosphere, but it is quite thin. The spacecraft landing on Mars requires a heat shield to absorb the heat generated while slowing down from tens of thousands of kilometres to just hundreds of kilometres per hour within the upper atmosphere of Mars. Even though the atmosphere is thin on Mars, the friction forces raise the temperature to over 1,200 degrees Centigrade, which is more than enough to burn any unprotected spacecraft. So, a heat shield that absorbs the heat is an essential part of any spacecraft landing on Mars.

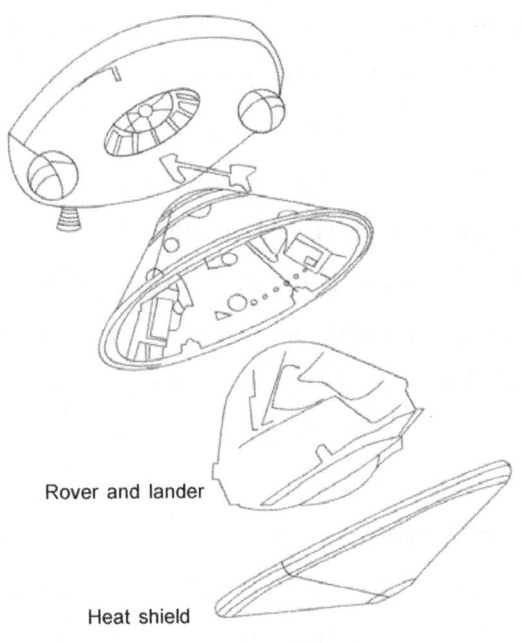

Rover and lander

Heat shield

Flight system

The rover gets safely through Mars' atmosphere and onto the surface with the help of the aeroshell, a parachute and airbags. The aeroshell has two parts: the heat shield that faces forward and a backshell. The parachute is attached to the backshell and opens to about 49 feet in diameter. The backshell also carries a meter to determine the right time for opening the parachute.

The airbags cushion the impact on the lander when it lands on the Martian surface. Each of the four faces of the folded-up lander is equipped with an envelope of six airbags stitched together. Gas generators are fitted to inflate the airbags. Each airbag has double bladders to take care of the pressure at impact. To protect the bladders from sharp rocks, there are six layers of a special cloth woven from a fibre material called Vectran, which is five times stronger than steel. Vectran is normally used for gutting in tennis racquets.

During the cruise stage solar panels on the cruise stage provide electricity for the spacecraft during the flight. Thrusters fitted on the cruise stage are fired to adjust the spacecraft's flight path three times during the cruise phase, and up to three more times during the final eight days of the approach phase.

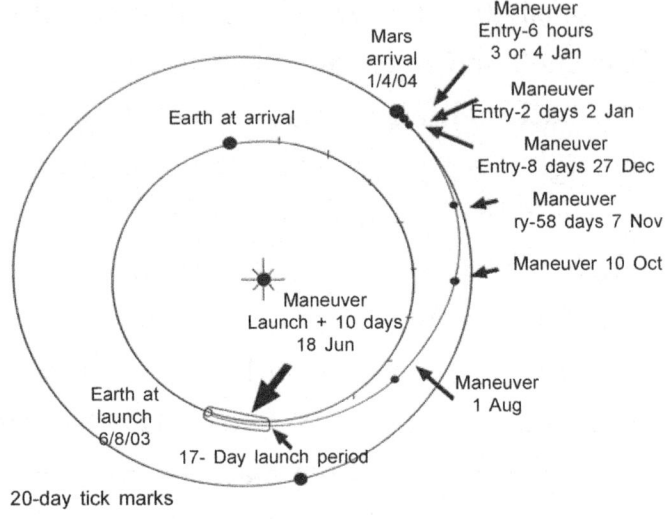

Flight path and maneuvers

Entry, descent and landing

About 76 minutes before entering Mars' atmosphere, the rover spacecraft turns to orient its shield forward. Fifteen minutes before the atmospheric entry, the protective aeroshell encasing the lander and rover separate from the cruise stage, whose role from that point is over.

The spacecraft hits the top of the atmosphere about 120 kilometres above Mars' surface at a velocity of 19,200 kilometres per hour. The friction of travelling through Mars' atmosphere heats and slows the spacecraft dramatically. Because of the heat, the surface of the heat shield can reach a temperature of 1,447 degrees Centigrade. Within four minutes after the atmospheric entry, the speed of the spacecraft decreases to about 1,536 kilometres per hour.

At this point (about 8.5 kilometres above the Martian surface), the spacecraft deploys its parachute. Within two minutes, the spacecraft bounces on the Martian surface, but those two minutes are packed with fast-paced events that decide whether the mission would be a success.

Twenty seconds after the deployment of the parachute, the spacecraft jettisons the bottom half of the protective shell, the heat shield, exposing the lander inside. Ten seconds later, the backshell, still attached to the parachute, begins lowering the lander on a string-like thing (bridle) about

66 feet long. Opening of the bridle to its full length takes about 10 seconds. Almost immediately, a radar system on the lander begins sending pulses towards the ground to measure the spacecraft's altitude. The radar starts detecting the ground when the spacecraft is about 2.4 kilometres above the surface (approximately 35 seconds before landing).

Eight seconds before the touchdown, the gas generators inflate the lander's airbags. Two seconds later, three rockets on the backshell, which are put there to slow down the spacecraft's descent, ignite. After three more seconds, when the lander is about 50 feet above the ground, the bridle is cut, releasing it from the backshell and parachute. The lander, which is protected by airbags, falls on the ground.

The first bounce when the lander falls on the ground takes it high above the ground. The bouncing and rolling of the lander last for several minutes. For example, Mars Pathfinder bounced about fifteen times, as high as 49 feet before coming to rest two and half minutes later at a distance of about a kilometre from where it had originally landed.

Twelve minutes after the landing, the motors begin retracting the airbags, a process which takes about an hour. Petals of the lander open only after that.

Surface operations

Opening of the four-sided lander uncovers the rover tucked inside. The rover's first action is to unfold its solar panels. Since the rover depends on sunlight to generate electrical power, the operations of the rover run on a schedule timed to the length of the Martian day. A Martian day, which is called *sol*, lasts 24 hours, 39 minutes and 35 seconds. After unfolding of the solar panels, the rover, still in a crouching position, starts taking images of the immediate surroundings with its four hazard-identification cameras mounted below the solar panels.

The rover now rises up from its crouching position and stands up to its full height while still on the lander's base petal. From its height, it takes a 360-degree colour panorama picture with its panoramic camera and a matching 360-degree panorama with its miniature thermal infrared spectrometer. The team on Earth relies heavily on these pictures to decide which rocks the rover should go to examine.

The rover now rolls off the lander. The lander's role in the mission ends with this. In the next few sols after its roll-off, the rover finishes checking its science instruments and moves to whichever nearby rock or patch of soils the science team on Earth has selected after analysing the panoramic and infrared pictures taken earlier by the rover.

To coordinate their work with the rover, the team on Earth will now change over to a Martian schedule. The forty-minute difference from the length of Earth's day means that, by about two weeks after the rover has landed on Mars' surface, the waking-up and meal times of the members of the science team would have shifted by about nine hours. The rover is designed to transmit each sol's accumulation of data early in the Martian afternoon. The science team will analyse that data, refine plans for the activity of the rover for the next sol and send commands accordingly to the rover.

The rover begins its day after a good night's sleep on being woken up by an alarm call. Instructions from Earth uploaded the previous day tell the rover how to carry out its operations for the day without any further communication from Earth. It is necessary that instructions from Earth should be sent the previous day. This is because the rover must enter the safe mode to maintain its systems during the freezing Martian nights.

The rover has to face its share of problems. These problems decide how long the rover will be in a position to continue working on Mars. During autumn in Mars, the intensity of solar radiation decreases and this lessens the amount of electrical power produced by the solar cells. In addition, the colder nights increase the need for electrically powered heating to keep the batteries warm enough to work. On top of this, there is plenty of dust on the Martian surface, and the accumulation of dust on the solar panels limit the life of the rover.

If the description of the rover makes it sound almost like a living thing, it is because scientists spend so much time working with them that these robots become almost like pets. And just like pets, the rovers get names that often say a lot about their personality. For example, Pathfinder mission's rover was called Sojourner in honour of an African-American reformist called Sojourner (actual name Isabella Van Wagener) who had made it her mission to travel up and down the land advocating rights for all during the US Civil War. The name for the rover was suggested by a twelve-year-old girl called Valerie Ambrose as part of a nation-wide competition.

The names Spirit and Opportunity were selected from a student essay contest that drew nearly 10,000 entries. Curiosity got its name from Clara Ma, a sixth grader. As part of her prize, Clara Ma signed her name on the rover before it was packed away for its journey to Mars.

Let's now recount the story of these four rovers—Sojourner, Spirit, Opportunity and Curiosity—and their expeditions to Mars.

Sojourner

On 4 July 1997, the Pathfinder mission landed on Mars. It had actually landed in a terrain full of rocks and yet the airbags had survived without a single puncture. The lander petals of Pathfinder opened and the tiny rover Sojourner emerged, undamaged.

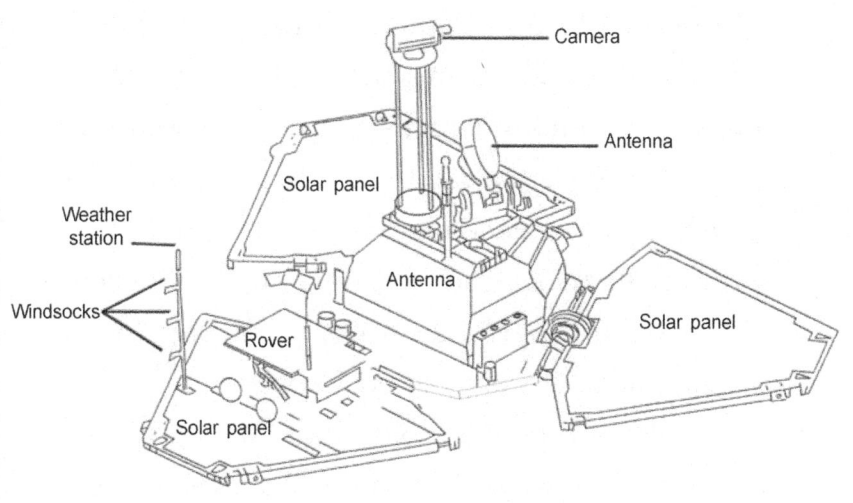

Mars Pathfinder

With two ramps available on Pathfinder, the rover should have had a choice of routes to roll down to the Martian surface. Unfortunately, the front raft could not touch the ground because part of the airbag assembly had not retracted fully. So on July 5 or sol 2 of its Martian life, Sojourner lifted itself up on all its six wheels and drove down the rear ramp to begin its ninety-sol excursion on the Martian surface.

Pathfinder had landed on Ares Vallis. From the first images sent by the lander to Earth, it could be seen that there was a large collection of loose rocks and boulders lying at the landing site. The science team on Earth, realizing that there were enough rocks there for Sojourner to analyse, decided to call the landing place the Rock Garden. The science team also gave names to the prominent rocks and boulders such as Barnacle Bill, Couch, Yogi and so on, according to their resemblances to objects on Earth.

It so happened that that the arrival of Sojourner on Mars became a big Internet event. A home page with rapid updating was set up

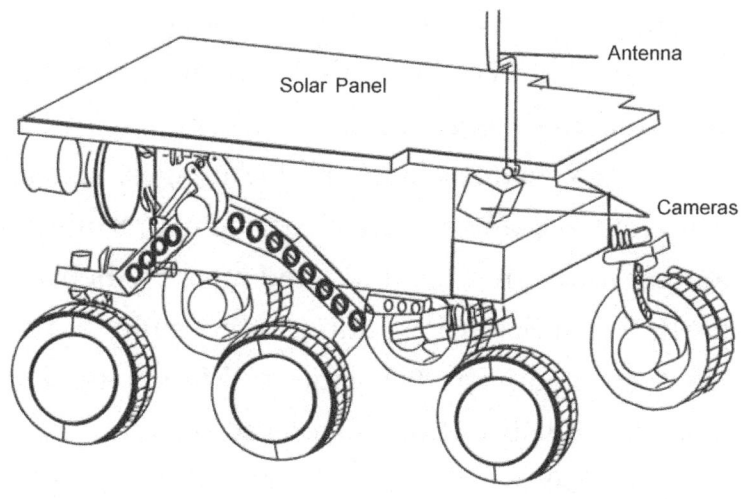

Sojourner

for Sojourner. During the first month itself, it got more than 560 million hits; the record for one day was 47 million hits. Never had a planetary probe got so much publicity.

When the rocks and boulders in the Rock Garden got their names, it became a fascinating event for the public. People become familiar with the site and even with individual rocks and boulders. For the first time, the public became interested in places and objects on Mars along with the team carrying out the mission.

Over a period of ninety-two sols, Sojourner went around the Rock Garden taking images and making measurements. Along with its lander, it sent back over 17,000 images, sixteen complete rock and soil analyses and over 8 million temperature, pressure and wind measurements to Earth. What Sojourner found in those ninety-two sols provided important clues to Mars' past. The analysis of distribution of rocks across the surface showed that a massive flood in the distant past had deposited these rocks there.

Sojourner functioned for a period that was three times longer than expected. But, with its batteries failing, the lander ceased communications with Earth on 27 September 1997.

Spirit

The Spirit rover landed on Mars on 4 January 2004. It bounced about 28 feet high when it touched the ground. After twenty-seven more bounces and then rolling, it came to a stop about 330 yards from the point of its first impact. Interestingly, though Spirit had travelled 487 million kilometres from the time it was launched, it landed only 10 kilometres from the place where it was supposed to land.

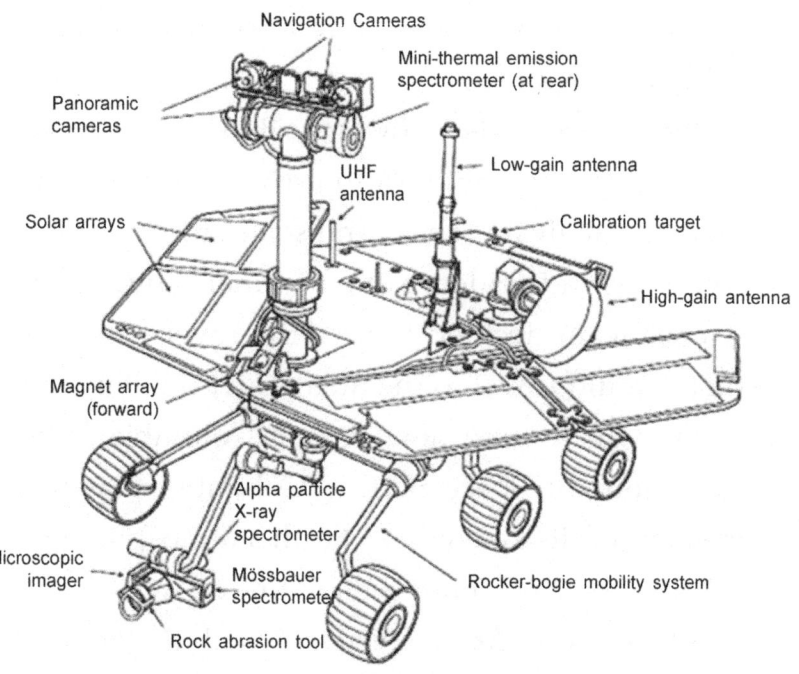

Mars Exploration Rover (Spirit/Opportunity)

Spirit landed in the middle of a gigantic crater. Situated south of Mars' equator, the crater was about 150 kilometres wide. After checking all its equipment and making sure that they were working, Spirit started its journey on sol 12 to find evidence of past water on Mars. Some 300 metres to the northwest of its landing site, there was a crater called Bonneville, and rising 100 metres above Bonneville crater were a set of hills about 2.5 kilometres away.

Spirit proceeded towards Bonneville crater and took sixty-eight sols to arrive there. It spent nine sols analysing rocks and soil in the crater but could not find evidence of past water activity. The science team decided to turn the rover round so that it could travel to the hills nearly 3 kilometres away, which were now named Columbia Hills, in honour of Space Shuttle Columbia that had crashed on its re-entry to Earth's atmosphere on 1 February 2003, killing its entire crew.

On 4 June 2004, Spirit reached the foot of Columbia Hills and struck gold. One of the first rocks that it analysed, called Pot of Gold, revealed the presence of hematite, which indicated the existence of past water. Some rocks that Spirit examined seemed to have been spoiled, while some others contained thin mineral rinds, which were all signs of past water activity. From June till late August 2004, Spirit climbed up Columbia Hills towards a point called West Spur, and its investigations indicated significant water activity billions of years ago affecting the entire area of Columbia Hills.

Around this time, Spirit had a problem with its body: its front right wheel stopped working. To continue its operations, the rover was turned around and driven backwards up the hills while it dragged its front wheel. During February 2005, Spirit travelled upwards to a point called Larry's Lookout, where it was able to look north into a neighbouring valley. Dust in the area revealed iron sulfate salts with water molecules bound to them. Spirit also found rocks that were rich in phosphorus. March 2005 was a good month for Spirit. The dust, which had gathered on its solar panels and reduced its power, was blown off by the high winds, increasing its power level. In addition, the faulty front right wheel started working.

Spirit, healthy once again, travelled to the summit of one of the hills, now named Husband

Hill. The seven peaks of Columbia Hills were named after seven members of the Columbia crew, with Husband Hill named in honour of Rick Husband, the Commander of the Columbia crew. Spirit reached the summit of Husband Hill on 21 August 2005 after having travelled a distance of 4 kilometres. On the summit of Husband Hills, there was a strong gust of wind that blew the remaining dust from the solar panels of Spirit, restoring full powers to the panels at 965 watts.

On 20 November 2005, there was a firework display in the form of a meteor shower caused by the dust from the tail of Halley's comet burning up in the atmosphere, and Spirit was there to take pictures of the display. It was befitting because on that day, Spirit had completed one Martian year (669 sols) on Mars. The team on Earth decided to send Spirit down towards a point called Home Plate. But Spirit's front wheel had started giving trouble again, finally failing in March 2006. So, Spirit rested on the slope of Columbia Hills and spent the entire Martian winter there.

When spring came to Mars that year, Spirit resumed its journey. It was still dragging its faulty front wheel. On its way to Home Plate, the rover discovered the best evidence of past water activity in Gusset Crater almost by accident. It scooped out some soil from the surface and found that it contained silicate salts of more than 90 per cent purity. Such deposits were certainly caused by past water activity. On Earth, such deposits are caused by volcanic stream or a hot spring.

Spirit went on exploring Mars for many more years before it fell silent after getting stuck while exploring a mountain in 2009. It had been given ninety sols for its mission but it had worked for five years. It had far exceeded all expectations.

Opportunity

Opportunity arrived on Mars on 24 January 2004, twenty days after Spirit. While landing on the Martian surface, it bounced twenty-six times and travelled about 220 yards from where it had landed. Finally it came to rest inside a small crater.

The crater in which Opportunity had landed was named Eagle crater. It was a small crater by Martian standards: about 72 feet in diameter and 10 feet deep. But Opportunity could not have landed in a better place. The sub-surface bedrock of the surrounding plain was clearly exposed on the walls of the crater. Here was a fabulous opportunity for the rover to analyse the sub-surface of Mars without having to do any drilling. The rover Opportunity had justified the name given to it.

Opportunity spent the best part of the next six weeks examining the walls of the Eagle crater. The rover found that the walls had sedimentary-layered rock, laid down by a standing body of water. As the wall had multiple layers, it was clear that the area had undergone multiple episodes of water flooding over long periods of time in the distant past. Opportunity also found small blue spheres of hematite lying on the floor of the crater and on its sides. When the rocks were chemically analysed, it was found that there were a number of salts which could only have been produced and then deposited by water.

These marble-sized spheres that Opportunity had found actually looked more grey than blue. But they looked so blue in the pictures taken by Opportunity that the science team on Earth came to the conclusion that the spheres looked like blueberries in a muffin, and the name stuck. The side of the Eagle crater where Opportunity had discovered the blueberries was named as the Berry Bowl.

After Opportunity spent fifty-seven sols exploring Eagle crater, it went off to a much larger crater called Endurance. It spent six months looking at Endurance crater. As it went deeper into the crater, there was strong evidence that water alteration had occurred in the past. By early 2005, Opportunity had got enough evidence to suggest that a shallow body of standing water had covered tens of thousands of square kilometres across Meridian Planum — the area where both Eagle and Endurance craters are located — for at least hundreds of thousands of years.

Opportunity now travelled to an even larger crater called Victoria, located about 4 kilometres south of Endurance crater. The journey was on a smooth terrain covered by shallow sand dunes. Unfortunately, Opportunity got stuck in the sand. For over five weeks, it struggled to extricate itself from the sand. After a long struggle, it managed to escape from the sand trap, and the team on Earth named this sand trap as Purgatory Dune.

While it travelled to Victoria crater, Opportunity found even better evidence of past water activity in the region. In December 2005, the rover had to make a service stop at a rocky outcrop called Olympia because the team on Earth tried to carry out a remotely controlled repair of its failing robotic arm. The joints on the robotic arm were beginning to stick, and the arm was not able to stow itself in the position required for the rover to travel.

When Opportunity stopped for the service break, the team noticed a feature called festoon cross-bedding within the rocks of Olympia. Such cross-bedding looks like small curved ripples within the rock and can only happen when surface running water is there. Here, finally, was firm evidence of surface liquid water having once flowed on Mars.

The team on Earth solved the problem of the robotic arm and Opportunity started travelling again. On the route, it visited a small crater called Erebus. The rocks in Erebus had festoon cross-bedding as well as pavement-type rocks formed from water percolating through cracks of the surface above. Opportunity spent the next four months looking at Erebus crater.

After looking at Erebus, Opportunity resumed its journey to Victoria and arrived there at a point named Duck Bay in September 2006. For the next eight months, the rover travelled on the rim of the crater in a clockwise direction. In May 2007, it turned back to Duck Bay. The Victoria crater provided a lot of information. The crater bared about 15 metres of layered rocks, which were far deeper than either in Eagle or Endurance crater. So Opportunity could gather details of Mars that spanned a greater period of the planet's past.

Today, Opportunity is still travelling on the surface of Mars. Opportunity's life was designed only for three months, but it is still going strong nine years later. Unfortunately, the rover's two mineralogical instruments do not work any more. But Opportunity has given us so much data that scientists on Earth will spend years analysing it. In any case, the rover has already provided sufficient evidence of past surface water on Mars.

Curiosity

Curiosity was launched on 26 November 2011. After an eight-month journey, it landed on Mars on 6 August 2012. Curiosity is over five times heavier than either Spirit or Opportunity,

While all the previous Mars rovers had a similar landing strategy, Curiosity's landing on Mars was the first of its kind. This was because of two major technological innovations that enabled Curiosity to do better than the previous rovers. One was the sky crane, a landing system that functions like an army helicopter lowering a vehicle to the surface. The other technological first was the active guidance device with an aerodynamic lift, a combination that allowed Curiosity to fly, rather than just fall, through the Martian atmosphere.

In the Curiosity mission, the spacecraft was packed into a shell that protected it during its journey to Mars and during its descent to the surface of the planet. As the shell holding the spacecraft zoomed to the surface of Mars at about 1,440 kilometres per hour, a parachute—the biggest ever built for a space mission—was released. The parachute acted like brakes to slow the spacecraft down. The spacecraft's protective shell fell away and the active guidance device holding the rover fired its eight jets and released Curiosity on the sky crane. The entire operation took about seven minutes.

These seven minutes have come to be known in the vocabulary of space flight as the 'seven minutes of terror'. This is because Curiosity had a complicated descent and landing operation, involving the deployment of a very large supersonic parachute and heat shield separation. But everything went off smoothly, and it was a great technological feat. Curiosity landed with amazing precision, touching down less than 2.4 kilometres from its target after a journey of 563 million kilometres.

Precision in the landing of Curiosity was important because the landing site chosen was a very tight area. Aeolis Palus in Gale crater, the chosen landing site, contains an 18,000-feet high mountain about 12 kilometres south of the landing site. It was necessary that Curiosity should not land on the mountain. The location where Curiosity touched down is now called Bradbury Landing after Ray Bradbury, the famous science fiction writer.

The 'seven minutes of terror' of the Curiosity landing was televised live, and millions of viewers on Earth watched it. Around 1,000 people gathered in the Times Square of New York City to watch NASA's live broadcast of Curiosity's landing, as footage was shown on the giant screen. Live video showing of the first footage from the surface of Mars was available on the Internet. Bobak Ferdowsi, the Flight Director for

Curiosity's landing, achieved Twitter celebrity status with 45,000 new followers subscribing to his Twitter account. His Mohawk hairstyle with yellow stars, which he wore during the televised broadcast contributed vastly to his popularity!

There was a big difference between the landing of Curiosity and the landing of the previous three rovers. Sojourner, Spirit and Opportunity became active only after the lander landed on the Martian surface and the petals of the lander opened, uncovering the rover tucked inside. Curiosity, on the other hand, had become active even before it actually touched down on the surface of Mars.

In fact, Curiosity became active when the sky crane was in the process of lowering it. After Curiosity had a soft landing on Mars, it waited for two seconds to confirm that it was on solid ground and fired several small explosive devices activating the cable cutters on the bridle to free itself from the spacecraft descent stage. The descent stage then flew away to a crash landing, and Curiosity started preparing itself to begin the next stage of its mission.

This stage of the Curiosity mission consists of exploring Mars to determine whether the Red Planet could have ever supported life and the role that water has played in it. It will also study the climate and geology of Mars. The mission will also help in preparing for a manned mission to the planet. The life of Curiosity is for one Martian year.

To help Curiosity in its mission, it is designed as a science laboratory. It is fitted with special instruments and cameras for doing various studies while on Mars. It has seventeen cameras, which will act as the rover's eyes, helping it to travel where it needs to go and investigate objects, rocks and soil. It also has ten science instruments to carry out tasks that scientists perform in a laboratory on Earth. So, instead of sending the samples back to Earth, Curiosity will do the laboratory tests right there on Mars.

Curiosity's task begins with its very powerful cameras looking for features of interest. If a particular surface is of interest, the rover uses its infrared laser to vapourize a small portion of the surface. This generates a spectral signature and the rover will examine the spectral signature to find out about the composition of the rock.

In some instances, the signature may not reveal necessary details about the composition of the rock. In that case, Curiosity will swing its robotic arm. The arm is a long one at 6.9 feet and holds five devices. Two of the devices are X-ray spectrometer and a camera called Mars Hand Lens Imager. The remaining three devices are a drill, a brush and a mechanism for scooping, sieving and portioning samples of powdered rock and soil.

Curiosity will also use its robotic arm for the X-ray spectrometer to take a closer look. If the specimen warrants further analysis, the drill on the arm will drill into the boulder and deliver a powdered sample to the Sample Analysis (SAM) lab or the Chemistry and Mineralogy (CheMin) lab, both of which are located inside the rover.

Gale crater, where Curiosity landed, is two billion years old. It was filled up by sediments first deposited by water and later deposited by wind. Over a period of time, gusts of wind blew away the surface sediments. Mount Sharp, which is 5.5

kilometres high, still has some of these sediments. So, Curiosity will have the opportunity to study two billion years of Martian history in the sediments exposed in Mount Sharp.

For about a month after it landed on Mars, Curiosity was parked at a sand dune where it was busy scooping up soil, sniffing the atmosphere and measuring the radiation levels on the surface. It has already examined the sedimentary settlements and seen some signs of water that flowed in the past through Gale crater. It has also analysed a small sample of the Martian air and detected a few parts per billion of methane.

Curiosity has also spotted something on a rock's surface that has been described as the 'Martian flower'. The 'Martian flower' is seen in images captured by Curiosity in December 2012. In the image, pearl-coloured petals appear to sprout from a rock's surface. According to NASA scientists, the cluster that looks like a flower is part of the rock itself.

Curiosity is now travelling to Mount Sharp to examine the rocks there. Great things are expected of Curiosity. After all, with its high-tech suite of instruments, it is the most sophisticated spacecraft to ever land on the Red Planet.

Robot Hedgehog

For future robotic missions, scientists are now designing a robotic rover called Robot Hedgehog. It is spherical in shape, about half a metre wide and covered with spikes. It is being designed to explore the surface of Phobos, one of the moons of Mars. The robot is spiky because spikes will help it to cope with rolling and hopping across the surface of Phobos.

Building a rover to rove on the surface of Phobos is a big challenge because it has very low gravity. The gravity of Phobos is only one-hundredth that of Earth. This makes getting around on wheels, treads or legs extremely difficult because the low gravity of Phobos means little or no traction.

The robot is made up of many facets covered in solar panels and spikes. Inside the shell of the Robot Hedgehog are three rotating discs set at right angles to one another. As these discs spin, the spikes dig in, and the hedgehog rolls, hops, tumbles and bounds in 10-metre arcs over the surface. NASA is planning to send a Phobos Surveyor orbiting spacecraft to act as the mother ship for about six Robot Hedgehogs, which will be landing on the surface of Phobos. The orbiting spacecraft will be the size of a coffee table, powered by two solar panels.

The Phobos exploration mission will take up to three years including the two-year journey from Earth. Once at Phobos, the Surveyor orbiting spacecraft will take pictures from the orbit, mapping the moon's topography. It will then release one hedgehog rover to the surface of Phobos, one at a time several days apart, for carrying out close-up studies.

The hedgehog rover will be in the future, but exploration of Mars already done by the robotic rovers has given us a lot of insights. It will be interesting to find out what we have found about Mars so far, what it is like today and what it might tell us about itself in the years to come.

5
What Do We Know About Mars?

It looks as if we have discovered a new Mars through the space missions. Ever since Mariner 4 brought us the first close-up pictures of Mars in 1965, the Red Planet has been revealed as a planet that is familiar, and yet so very different. Spacecraft pictures have shown us that Mars is rocky, cold and barren beneath its pink sky. Like Earth, Mars has polar ice caps and clouds in the atmosphere, seasonal weather patterns, volcanoes, canyons and other recognizable features. But Mars is also an extreme planet and very different from Earth in several ways. What is Mars really like?

Mars is only about one-half the diameter of

Earth, but both the planets have the same amount of dry surface area. This is because oceans cover more than one-third of Earth's surface whereas the surface of Mars has no liquid water at present.

Gravity

The pull of gravity on an object on Mars is about two-fifth of the pull on the same object on Earth. So, an object on Mars will weigh two-fifth of its weight on Earth, but the object (mass) will remain the same. What it actually means is that we have to make less effort to lift objects on Mars. Weight is the pull of gravity on an object (mass), so weight changes with the pull of gravity of each planet. When humans go to live on Mars, they will need to adapt to the lower gravity of the planet.

Atmosphere

Mars has a very thin atmosphere. It is composed almost entirely of carbon dioxide (95 per cent). In that respect, it is like Venus. In contrast, Earth's atmosphere is mostly nitrogen (77 per cent) and oxygen (21 per cent). The thin atmosphere of Mars allows cosmic and solar radiation to hit the surface of the planet, making it difficult for life to survive. In contrast, Earth's thick atmosphere protects life on Earth from radiation.

The thin atmosphere of Mars has less than 1 per cent of the air molecules that Earth's atmosphere has. Since the atmosphere of Mars is composed mostly of carbon dioxide, human beings will find it difficult to breathe. But plants can certainly use carbon dioxide. There are trace gases in the atmosphere of Mars as well as a little water vapour that forms wispy clouds. The water vapour can freeze on rocks and soil forming white frost.

Dust storms

Very often, during the Martian spring, there are strong winds that stir up fine dust from the Martian surface. These dust storms fill the sky with gritty dust and sometimes cover the entire planet in a reddish cloud. The air near the planet's surface is warmed by the Sun and, just like on Earth, the warm air rises up, creating wind currents. Sometimes these wind currents cause swirling dust devils that travel across the Mars terrain. We can make out the tracks of these dust devils from the pictures taken by spacecraft. We see similar dust devils in dry deserts on Earth. Sometimes the force of the wind can be high on Mars but since the atmosphere is so thin there, the force of the wind can never be high as on Earth.

The dust carried by the winds affects the visibility of Mars from Earth. During seventeenth and eighteenth centuries, astronomers looking at Mars through their telescopes found dark and light areas changing frequently. We know now that the dust carried by the winds was to blame for this. For example, Syrtis Major, the first surface feature identified on Mars, appeared to be a dark area which people thought was a big sea. Actually the dark area that the astronomers saw is a plain area sloping gently upwards. For short periods, it is partly covered by light dust before the dust is blown away by the winds.

Sometimes, there are big dust storms on Mars. This usually happens when Mars is closest to the Sun and it is summer in the southern hemisphere. In certain areas there are small dust clouds all the time, but every now and then, the clouds gather to form the big storm that covers the entire planet. In fact, when Mariner 9 reached Mars' orbit, and two Soviet probes — Mars 2 and Mars 3 — were already there, they found that a big dust storm was in progress and they could see nothing of the Martian surface.

Mariner 9 was reprogrammed to wait for the dust to disperse, and the science team on Earth used the waiting time to photograph Phobos, a moon of Mars. But Mars 2 and Mars 3 could not be reprogrammed as their programmes had already been loaded prior to their launch and they could not be changed. So, Mars 2 and Mars 3 took photographs of Mars covered with thick dust.

Temperature

Mars is very cold. It is a planet of extreme temperatures: it can be up to -125 degrees Centigrade in the cold winter nights. Because the atmosphere is so thin, it cannot hold much of the Sun's warming rays, thus making the air much colder than the surface rocks on summer days. Another reason for Mars being colder than Earth is that it does not receive as much heat from the Sun since Mars is much further away from the Sun than Earth. There is also a lack of greenhouse effect on the planet.

Mars has seasons just like Earth. They are caused by the difference in the amount of the Sun's rays that hit the northern and southern hemispheres due to the tilt of the planet as it orbits the Sun. The seasons last longer on Mars, about twice as long as seasons on Earth. This is because Mars' orbit around the Sun takes twice as long as Earth's orbit.

The lengths of the seasons and weather conditions are different in the two hemispheres of Mars. Summer in the northern hemisphere and winter in the southern hemisphere last more than 180 sols. The length of winter in the northern hemisphere and summer in the northern hemisphere is just over 160 sols. The difference between spring and autumn is larger still, more than 60 sols. In the northern hemisphere, the winter is short and mild, and summer is long and cool. In the southern hemisphere, the winter is long and freezing cold, and the summer is short and temperate.

The tilt

One reason for the extreme seasonal changes in Mars is its wobbling axis of rotation. There is a large variation in Mars' axis tilt. For example, the Earth's axis is currently tilted at an angle of 23.5 degrees. The axial tilt of Earth varies between 22 and 24 degrees, whereas the axial tilt of Mars varies between 13 and 40 degrees.

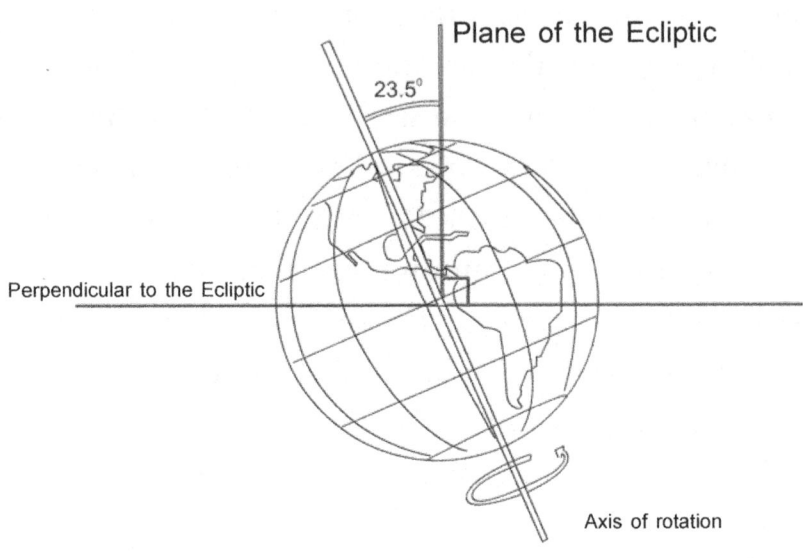

Plane of the Ecliptic

23.5°

Perpendicular to the Ecliptic

Axis of rotation

Earth's axial tilt

At present, Mars and Earth share a similar angle of axial tilt: Mars at 25 degrees and Earth at a fairly constant 23.5 degrees. During the last ten million years, Earth's axial tilt has only varied between about 22 and 24 degrees. This is because our large moon has helped Earth in maintaining a stable tilt. But Mars, which has two tiny moons, has experienced extreme changes in its axial tilt: between 13 and 40 degrees. At times when Mars' axial tilt is high, the summer polar cap points directly towards the Sun. This makes the ice melt or change from solid to gas.

Because of these fluctuations in axial tilt, many scientists believe that extreme changes in climate and seasons have occurred throughout Mars' history. These extreme changes would have included episodes of melting ice and water production. Calculations show that throughout the geologic history of Mars, its average axial tilt would have been about 40 degrees, and sometimes the tilt could have been as high as 80 degrees. During periods of high tilt, ice would have accumulated in the tropics rather than at the poles.

Difference between the hemispheres

One thing that is striking about Mars is the big difference between its southern and northern hemispheres. The northern hemisphere consists of low-lying plains. It is mostly flat with only a few craters. The southern hemisphere consists of highlands and is covered with craters. The southern hemisphere is much older than the northern hemisphere. Scientists think that Mars was subject to heavy impact early on in its formation. According to scientists, the collisions occurred in the first 100 million years of the formation of Mars and stripped the outer part of the northern hemisphere. Scientists estimate that an object half to two-thirds the size of Earth's moon struck early Mars at an angle of 30 to 60 degrees.

Landforms and terrains

If the idea is that humans will one day go to Mars and live there, it is necessary to identify and understand the wide variety of landforms and terrains that make up the geography of Mars. Scientists are doing that now. Of course, there are many familiar landforms on Earth that allow scientists to understand some of the processes that shape the surface of Mars. Scientists compare what we know about Earth with what the robotic rovers go and see on Mars, so that they can identify the geologic processes that are active now on Mars or were active in the past.

Volcanoes

Two of the major landforms that were identified from space probes are volcanoes and impact craters. There are many volcanoes on Mars, the largest of them being the Olympus Mons.

At 600 kilometres across and 21 kilometres high, Olympus Mons is the largest volcano in the solar system. It is about three times higher than the highest peak on Earth, Mount Everest. In contrast, the largest volcano on Earth, Mauna Loa, is 120 kilometres across and 9 kilometres high. Although Olympus Mons is very tall, the rise of its slope is so gradual that a climber will barely notice that the land is moving upwards.

Craters

Craters, which are holes in the ground caused by meteors and comets hitting Mars, dot the surface of the Red Planet. Some of the craters are huge like the Hellas basin—2,300 kilometres in diameter and 4 kilometres below the ground. There are also thousands of smaller craters that are found mostly in the highland region of the southern hemisphere.

Canyons and valleys

Mars has many canyons and valleys. These seem to have been formed by cracking in the planet's surface, when there was a movement in its crust. For example, the cracking uplifted a portion of Mars 11 kilometres above the ground. The resulting bulge, the Tharsis Rise, is roughly equivalent to the combined size of the United States and Canada. The uplift created stress on the surface causing it to rift and form fractures thousands of kilometres long and hundreds of kilometres wide. For reasons that are not fully understood by scientists, some of these fractures got enlarged into a 4,000 kilometre long system of canyons.

This group of canyons is called Valles Marineris, named in honour of the Mariner missions that explored Mars from the mid-1960s to the early 1970s. Valles Marineres is the largest canyon in the solar system. It is 4,000 kilometres long, up to 700 kilometres wide and as much as 10 kilometres deep. To get an idea of how big it is, one needs to compare it with the Grand Canyon, one of the most impressive canyons on Earth. The Grand Canyon, which spans 29 kilometres and is 1.8 kilometres deep, is a dwarf compared to Valles Marineris, which is so wide that a person standing on one edge would not be able to see the other side.

Moons

Mars has two small moons: Phobos and Deimos. Phobos means fear and Deimos means panic. They were named after the horses that pulled the chariot of the Greek war god Ares. These two moons have surface material similar to that of many asteroids, which leads most scientists to believe that Phobos and Deimos are captured asteroids. Both these moons are as old as the solar system.

These moons are blacker than coal and look like battered potatoes. Deimos, the outer of the two moons, is the smaller one. Both Phobos and Deimos have irregular shapes. Both have lots of craters caused by heavy bombardment. The battering that these two little bodies received from bombardment is partly responsible for their irregular shapes. The other reason is that these bodies are so small that gravity has not been able to pull them into a spherical shape.

The largest crater on Phobos, which is called Stickney, is 10 kilometres in diameter. The craters on Phobos resemble the craters on Mars, and make its surface look very rough. But on Deimos the craters are shallow and filled with dust. The dust that covers the surface of Deimos makes the terrain smooth like a blanket of snow.

Phobos orbits Mars in only 7 hours and 39 minutes. This is about a third of the rotational period of Mars. So, in the course of one sol, Phobos travels around Mars more than three times. It rises from the west, rapidly crosses the sky and sets some four hours later in the east.

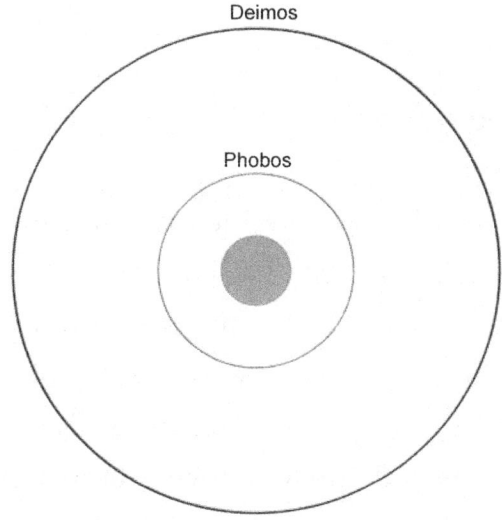

Orbits of Phobos and Deimos

The time that Deimos takes to orbit Mars is 30 hours and 21 minutes. It rises in the east and sets in the west. It moves very slowly. It takes a total of sixty hours—more than two sols—to travel across the sky. During that time Deimos has gone through its phases twice.

The small size of Phobos and Deimos means that gravity on both the moons is very weak. An astronaut standing on Phobos would be one thousand times lighter than on Earth. Any large jump might result in the astronaut flying off into space.

Unsolved mysteries

On the whole, we have learnt a lot about Mars from the space probes. We have made tremendous progress to date, but some important questions remain unanswered. One question is: is there life on Mars? Life requires water to survive. On Earth, we have found life wherever there is water. Is the same thing true of Mars? Because of the thin atmosphere and low temperatures of Mars today, we know that there is no liquid water on the surface. Was that always true? Information from space probes indicates that Mars was warmer and wetter once. If that is the case, did life ever arise on Mars? We need to know the answers to these questions.

6

Was There Water on Mars?

Water creates an environment that sustains and nurtures life. Early human settlements were established near rivers because they needed a nearby source of fresh water. Our planet Earth is unique in its abundance of liquid water. About 70 per cent of Earth's surface is covered with water. Water is the most fundamental component of Earth's environment and can be found in all its three states: solid, liquid and gas.

Was there water on Mars? Fifty years ago, everything we knew about Mars was based on what sketchy bits of information the astronomers could get by peering at it from telescopes on

Earth. Percival Lowell claimed that he had seen Mars criss-crossed by canals and waterways. That was only a guess and Lowell based it on what he thought he saw as narrow streaks on the surface of Mars.

We now know that Lowell's canals and waterways do not exist. Visions of a lush, water-soaked Mars vanished when Mariner 4 showed the planet to be barren and lifeless like our own Moon is. The Viking missions confirmed this. Mars as we came to know it is cold, nearly airless and bombarded by hostile radiation both from the Sun and from deep space.

But along the way since then, new truths have emerged. With their discovery of many geological forms that could have been formed only from large amounts of water, the Viking missions changed our ideas about the presence of water on Mars. They found big river valleys in many areas on Mars. These showed that there were huge floods of water on Mars, which had broken through dams and carved deep valleys, and the floodwater had travelled thousands of kilometres.

What the space probes found

Mars Global Surveyor carried an instrument called Thermal Emission Spectrometer (TES), which could detect the mineral composition on Mars. Mineral composition gives information about the presence or absence of water in ancient times. TES identified a large area that contained the mineral olvine. In the presence of water, olvine weathers into minerals such as goethite, chlorite, smectite, maghemite and hematite. Mars Global Surveyor charted the hematite deposits on Mars and found them in three places: Valles Marineris, Aram crater and Meridiani Planum. That is why Meridiani Planum was chosen as the landing site for the rover Opportunity.

The Spirit rover found hematite in Gusev crater in 2004. The existence of hematite is evidence of past water on the Red Planet. But the most convincing evidence came when Spirit found the mineral goethite. Goethite is conclusive proof for the existence of water because without water goethite will not form.

The Opportunity rover found blueberries of hematite in Eagle crater. The interior of blueberries is made of olivine. Scientists think that these blueberries were formed inside the stones from minerals in water. Later they were spread across the surface of Mars by strong winds. According to scientists, these minerals tell us that the region was covered with water that gradually evaporated and all that is left behind is a variety of minerals.

We have evidence on Earth that hematite is often formed in a wet environment, and deposits of hematite are found in areas where there was standing water or hot spring. Evidence of this is found in Yellowstone National Park of the United States. In southern Utah of the United States, similar features formed when minerals precipitated from groundwater seeped through Navajo sandstone millions of years ago. If the Martian blueberries formed in a similar fashion, then the vast plains where Opportunity found them must have had a wet history.

Mars Odyssey also found evidence of water.

One of the instruments that Odyssey carried was the Gamma Ray Spectrometer (GRS). GRS can measure gamma-ray radiation (cosmic radiation from space) coming from the surface of Mars and beneath it. When it hits Mars' surface, gamma-ray radiation releases neutrons that penetrate to a depth of 2 metres. At the same time, these neutrons hit atoms of different elements in the ground. This causes emission of more gamma-ray radiation, the properties of which can be used to deduce the elements it is emitted by.

Observations made by the GRS prove that there is a lot of hydrogen underneath the Martian surface, and it is hydrogen that, together with oxygen, makes molecules of water. In addition, pictures taken by Odyssey support the idea that Mars once had great amounts of water flowing across its surface. Some pictures show patterns of branching valleys. Others show layers that might have formed under lakes.

One of the first observations made by the Mars Reconnaissance Orbiter was that water did flow through underground rocks in ancient Mars. The

Orbiter took many pictures that suggest that Mars has had a rich history of water-related processes. A major discovery was finding evidence of hot springs. These hot springs may have contained life and may now contain well-preserved fossils of life.

Scientists looking at pictures sent by the Viking missions found signs of an ancient coastline that may have marked the edges of a long-lost sea. Based on this, some scientists suggested that there was an ocean on Mars once upon a time. Measurements based on the findings of the Mars Global Surveyor revealed two unbroken formations looking like shorelines. If there was an ocean, it has a billion-year-old past, with the surface of Mars going through all kinds of changes during that time.

Some scientists think that the floodwater coming from the southern hemisphere gave rise to the ocean. Other scientists think that it was the ocean that caused the great floods on Mars. With the climate getting cooler, the ocean would have got an ice cover and its weight would have squeezed the water still in liquid form toward the south, below the ground.

There is no doubt that liquid water once flowed on the surface of Mars. For the first 500 million years in the history of Mars, there were rivers and lakes, and perhaps an ocean covering a large portion of the surface of the planet. At the age of about 1 billion years, the conditions on the planet began to change. The atmosphere dwindled, the climate cooled, and the water disappeared. All that was left was a Martian terrain with a record of water having flowed there a long time ago.

Most space probes have sent back pictures that show evidence of features like dry riverbeds, ancient shorelines, vast flood plains, water-carved valleys and gullies. All of these indicate that there was liquid water in Mars at some point of time. Scientists believe that all these features came into existence millions of years ago when Mars was wetter and warmer.

What the geographical features tell us

Scientists at Brown University in the United States have found a gully fan system on Mars that formed about 1.25 million years ago. It shows signs of water activity on the Red Planet. The fan offers evidence that it was formed by liquid water that originated in nearby snow and gullies. In a research paper that appeared in the 2009 March issue of *Geology*, scientists of Brown University were able to date the gully system and give reasons for the presence of water.

Scientists working at the Planetary Science Institute in Arizona and the Georgia Institute of Technology have come up with an interesting conclusion. According to them, clay minerals — that usually form when water is present for long periods of time — cover a large portion of Mars. Presence of clay mineral has been identified by using a spectroscopic analysis from the Mars Reconnaissance Orbiter.

Clay exists in Meridiani Planum, the vast plain just south of the equator, which Opportunity rolled over as it trekked towards its current position. Opportunity did not find clay in Meridiani Planum because the science team on Earth controlling the rover did not know at that time that clay existed on Mars. Opportunity has now reached an area that scientists believe has rich clay deposits, but the rover will not be able to explore the area for clay. That is because both the mineralogical instruments of Opportunity do not work any more.

What these scientists say about clay deposits on Mars will be important to determine whether there was water on Mars at some point of time. Scientists point out that clay in Mars is a product of how the quality of water has changed. Clay formed when the water had alkali. When water became acidic, sulfates (a kind of salt) formed.

The Black Beauty

As a result of some cosmic collisions, pieces of Martian rocks were thrown into space, and they ultimately landed on Earth. About sixty-five of these rocks from Mars have been found on Earth. They have been found either in Antarctica or the Sahara desert. The oldest of these rocks dates back 4.5 billion years to a time when Mars was wetter and warmer. Only about half a dozen of these Martian rocks are 1.3 billion years old while all others are 600 million years old or even younger.

The latest rock to be found is NWA7034. It is also called 'Black Beauty' because it has the same colour as that of coal. It is very small and can be held in one's hands. It was found in the Sahara desert. An American bought it from a Moroccan meteorite dealer and donated it to the University of New Mexico.

Scientists conducted a number of tests on the Black Beauty. Based on its chemical signature, they concluded that it is from Mars. Scientists also found that it is 2.1 billion years old, and is the second oldest Martian meteorite that formed from a volcanic eruption. This rock is strikingly similar to the volcanic rocks examined on the Martian surface by Spirit and Opportunity which contain water-bearing minerals.

Where did the water go?

So there is enough evidence that Mars had water in the past, at least on the surface. What happened to that water? Some of the water could have been frozen in the Martian soil. Water frozen in the soil is called ground ice. If the ground ice remains throughout the year without melting, it is called permafrost. Permafrost is common in places like Siberia, northern Canada and near peaks of high mountains on Earth.

Mars is as cold or colder than the coldest place here on Earth. Ground ice on Mars should stay frozen throughout the year, and will be permafrost. However, finding the ground ice on Mars is not easy. A dry layer of soil is believed to be on top of the icy soil, making it difficult to detect it at the surface.

Scientists who study Mars have thought of several ways to search for permafrost on Mars. Some are looking at the pictures of the surface of Mars taken by orbiting spacecraft like Mars Global Surveyor and hope to find features similar to those made by permafrost here on Earth, including wedge-shaped cracks on the ground that meet to form multi-sided shapes and look a lot like giant mud cracks.

Another way of finding ground ice is to send a probe below the surface of Mars. Many scientists think that close to the Martian polar region, the dry layer of soil will be very thin, and the icy ground will be close to the surface. The Mars Polar Lander was designed to land on the surface of Mars near the southern pole in 1999. It carried Deep Space 2, a mini probe that was designed to penetrate up to about 3 feet into the soil and send information from below the ground. Unfortunately, the Mars Polar Lander was destroyed while attempting a landing. The probe Deep Space 2 was also lost in the process.

Answering the question of what happened to water on Mars is important to scientists for many reasons. Water is related to the climate of Mars and finding ground ice could help scientists understand how the climate of Mars has changed over time. Is there life in Mars below the ground?

Knowing how much water Mars had in the past and what has happened to that water will help scientists answer this question.

Someday, humans will go to Mars. If they want to live on Mars, it is important to know how much frozen water there is in the Martian ice sheets. This is exactly what the MARSIS radar instrument on Mars Express Orbiter is doing now. In order to measure the thickness of ice sheets in the polar region, the radar instrument sends signals to the surface and records the echoes. In this way, the radar is able to see through the layers to the bottom of the ice. Mars Express Orbiter has made more than 300 of these slices through the deposits of ice and dust that cover the polar region. It has found that the southern ice cap is up to 3.7 kilometres thick and the northern ice cap is about 1.8 kilometres thick. If all that ice ever melts, an ocean 11 metres thick would cover the entire Red Planet.

NASA has chalked out an exploration strategy called 'Follow the Water'. The strategy of following the water starts with an understanding of the current environment on Mars. NASA scientists want to explore features like dry riverbeds, ice in the polar caps and the kind of rocks that form only when water is present. They want to look for hot springs or water reserves below the ground. They want to find out if ancient Mars had a vast ocean. On the whole, scientists would like to understand how the change came about from a wet and warm Mars to the dry and dusty climate it has today.

7

Is There Life on Mars?

In July 1976, the Viking mission was taking photographs of Mars to find a suitable landing site for its lander. The photograph of the plains of Cydonia Planitia showed a shape resembling a human face. NASA published the photograph to tell the public about the interesting features the spacecraft had found on the surface of Mars.

This photograph came to be known as the 'Face of Mars'. Some people think that it not only looks like a human face, but it is that of a Martian, and that too, of the local ruler of Cydonia Planitia. According to them, a huge monument—2.5 kilometres long and 250 metres high—had been built on Mars to honour the ruler.

In April 1998, Mars Global Surveyor photographed the place where the Viking mission had found the Face. But by then it had disappeared. People think that the real explanation for the missing 'Face of Mars' lies in a dark conspiracy. According to them, Mars Observer, the probe which was lost in 1992, was not actually lost, but did what it was supposed to do: it was sent to photograph the Face. After acquiring evidence that an ancient civilization had existed there, the probe destroyed the monument with a nuclear bomb.

There is no consensus on what the truth really is. There are numerous websites on the Internet dedicated to Martian conspiracy theories. Google comes up with 1.5 million hits for Cydonia Planitia in one-tenth of a second. This only means that there are a lot of people on Earth who still believe what astronomers in the nineteenth century said: that Mars has life.

In the late nineteenth century, Schiaparelli and Percival Lowell saw straight lines criss-crossing the surface of Mars. To Lowell, it appeared as if these lines joined green areas that were covered by vegetation. Lowell thought that the straight lines were canals built by Martians to carry water to their crops. Not everyone was sure about an intelligent race of Martians building such a large network of canals and waterways to bring water to their crops. But it was common belief that there may be some kind of life on the Red Planet, or at least some form of vegetation. This was the belief that held sway till the 1960s.

Since then, pictures brought to us by space probes have shown that these canals and waterways carrying water to plants do not exist. There is no sign of life on the surface of Mars: neither plants nor intelligent Martians.

The Viking landers, which landed on Mars in July and September of 1976, carried biological laboratories to the surface of Mars. The idea was to settle, once and for all, the question of life on Mars. But these landers could not provide any final answers because the results of the tests they conducted were contradictory.

The pictures sent by Mariner 9 showed distinct signs of water having existed on Mars in the past.

Other spacecraft probes revealed that there are large areas of water ice at the polar caps. There is a lot of ice in the frozen ground. Large, dry channels also show that there was once a lot of running water on the surface. Recent results from Mars Express show that there may be liquid water deep underground.

Among our discoveries about Mars, one discovery stands out: the presence of liquid water on Mars in its ancient past or below the surface. Water is important because almost everywhere we find water on Earth, we find life. If Mars once had liquid water, or still does today below the surface, we need to ask whether any microscopic life forms could have developed in Mars. If Mars was once warmer and wetter, life may have begun on the Red Planet. Simple life, such as bacteria, may still exist beneath the frozen Martian surface.

Pieces of Mars on Earth

In 1996, a group of scientists announced that pieces of Mars had arrived on Earth as a meteorite and these pieces contain evidence pointing to the possible existence of life early in the history of the Red Planet. The meteorite that contains these pieces of Mars is called ALH84001 and was found in Antarctica. ALH84001 is named after the place where it was found — Allan Hills in Antarctica.

According to scientists, ALH84001 was lying on Mars for 500 million years till a large meteorite hit it. The impact of the hit caused the stone to melt partially. After that it lay on Mars for another 4 billion years. Then, some 15 million years ago, a new impact threw the stone out into space. Only about 13,000 years ago, it plunged into Earth's atmosphere and came to rest in Antarctica.

There are several things about ALH84001 that excite scientists. One is that it contains a lot of small grains of mineral formations consisting of carbon, oxygen and a few other elements. They are very much like certain organisms living in the seas on Earth.

These grains have compounds that usually form in the decomposition of living organisms or in barbecuing meat. The iron oxide and iron sulphide crystals present in these grains are just like what is produced by some primitive bacteria on Earth. In addition, the edges of the grains contain microscopic oblong structures that look remarkably like single-cell bacteria.

A team consisting of scientists from NASA and UK Open University analysed ALH84001. When the results of their analysis were announced, it created a sensation.

The team declared that it had uncovered evidence of life from Mars within this meteorite. Powerful microscope images showed what appeared to be fossilized bacteria within the meteorite. Magnetite mineral, which was discovered nearby, was consistent with waste material from the bacteria. Moreover, there was organic material within the fossil that could have come from once-living organisms within the rock.

Methane

The discovery of methane gas in Mars has also been an important breakthrough. The data sent by Mars Express Orbiter indicates that there are tiny amounts of methane gas in the atmosphere of Mars. The amounts of methane may be very small but what is interesting is that methane gas has been there over a period of time. Normally, solar radiation would have broken up the methane into carbon dioxide, and the gas would have disappeared. So, if there is methane in Mars' atmosphere over a period of time, it means that new methane is being produced continuously. Scientists think that the continuous presence of methane on Mars can only be explained by the fact that it may be coming from living organisms.

There are many scientists who think that this kind of evidence is not enough to prove the existence of life on Mars. True, all these do not conclusively prove it, but it does not exclude the possibility of existence of life either. Obviously more evidence is needed, and more evidence will come our way only when we send more probes to Mars. That is why it is necessary that Mars should be explored regularly.

8
India's Mission to Mars

The Indian Space Research Organisation (ISRO) is planning to send a mission to Mars in October 2013. It is named the Mars Orbiter Mission (MOM). This will be ISRO's first mission to Mars with a spacecraft designed to orbit Mars in an elliptical orbit.

Exploring space to advance knowledge of the Universe has always been an important part of the Indian space programme. India's solar system exploration programme was initiated in a major way in October 2008 with the launch of Chandrayaan 1, the first lunar mission of India. Chandrayaan 1 carried eleven payloads and was designed as a polar orbiter to map the surface chemistry, mineralogy and the particle radiation movement of the Moon. The major contribution of Chandrayaan 1 was the discovery of water on the lunar surface.

It was a proud day for India when the Moon Impact Probe carrying the Indian tricolour touched the south polar region of the Moon. The success of Chandrayaan 1 mission firmly established that India could take on any technological challenge. It created a new sense of confidence in India's ability to reach the frontiers of space exploration.

After the first lunar mission, ISRO is now working on a lunar landing mission, Chandrayaan 2. It consists of an orbiter, a lander and a rover. Chandrayaan 2 is designed to carry out several scientific studies using a suite of five experiments in the orbiting spacecraft.

India's mission to Mars is primarily to prove ISRO's technological capability of sending a mission to Mars. It is also a science mission because it is designed to carry out observations of the physical features of Mars and do a study of the Martian atmosphere with five scientific payloads.

Launch vehicle

The Mars orbiter spacecraft will be launched by Polar Satellite Launch Vehicle (PSLV-XL). PSLV is a world-class vehicle. PSLV flights have placed a number of satellites in precise orbits. PSLV has a history of twenty-two successful launches. It was a PSLV-XL rocket that carried the Chandrayaan 1 spacecraft to the Moon.

PSLV-XL is a four-stage vehicle. It is 44 metres tall and has a diameter of 2.8 metres. It can lift a mass of 320 tonnes. The first and third stages use solid motors. The second and fourth stages use liquid engines. Up to six solid motors can be attached to the core stage based on mission requirement. Four of the strap-on motors are ignited on the ground with the remaining two ignited in flight depending on requirement.

A rocket engine produces thrust by burning fuel (propellant) and expelling gas out of the engine. Propellant includes both fuel and oxidiser. The fuel is the chemical that rockets use to burn, but for the burning to take place, an oxidiser (oxygen) must be present. Solid motors use solid propellant, which is a mixture of oxidiser, fuel and other ingredients bound together. In the case of liquid engines, the propellant and oxidiser are put in separate tanks. One tank carries the fuel such as kerosene or liquid hydrogen. The other tank carries oxidiser such as liquid oxygen. The fuel and oxidiser are combined inside a cavity called the combustion chamber.

The trajectory

The PSLV rocket will take the MOM spacecraft and put it in Earth's orbit. The spacecraft will then be given higher speed to escape the gravitational force of Earth. The point at which it escapes is called the Earth's sphere of influence (SOI). After that, the spacecraft will be in the cruise stage. After 294 days, it will reach Mars' sphere of influence (Mars SOI) and will start orbiting around Mars. The Earth-Mars trajectory for the MOM spacecraft is shown below.

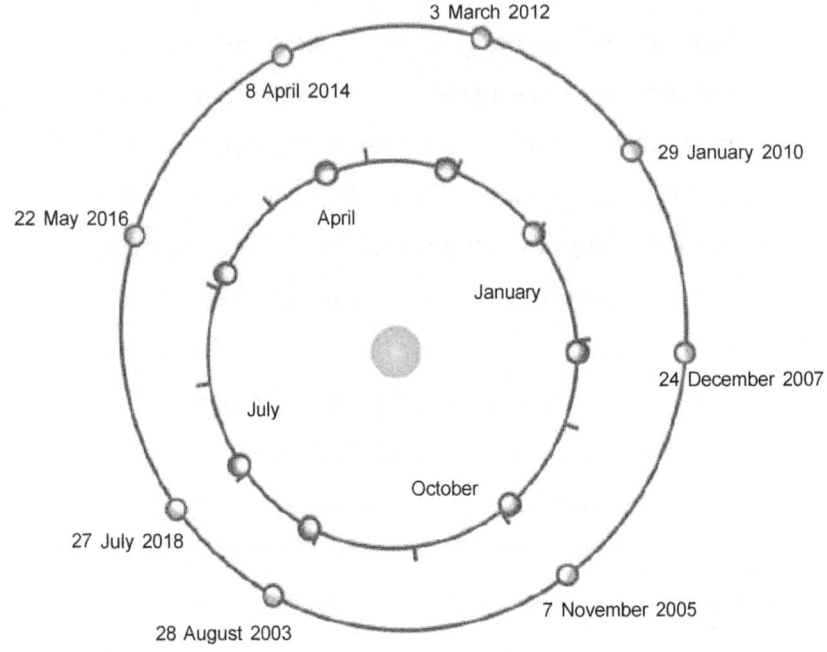

Interplanetary Transfer Trajectory

Launch opportunity

Every twenty-six months Earth and Mars return to approximately the same position with respect to each other. Hence, launch windows to Mars arise only every twenty-six months.

Present optimum opportunities are in the years 2013, 2016 and 2018. For ISRO's maiden mission

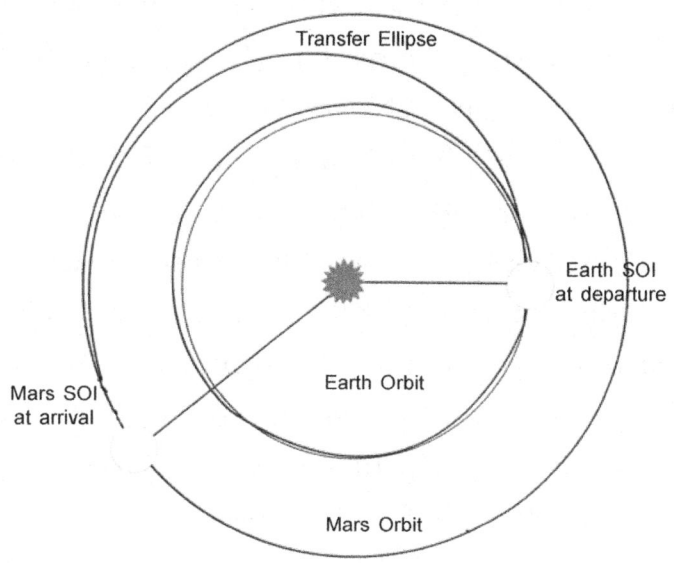

to Mars, the 2013 opportunity with PSLV launch has been selected. The optimum departure date — the day of performing the Trans-Mars Injection (TMI) manoeuvre to achieve the desired escape trajectory — is 27 November 2013.

Mission sequence

ISRO has worked out a detailed mission sequence, with 22 October 2013 as the launch date. The launch date has to be in October because of weather constraints. After the TMI on 27 November 2013, the spacecraft will cross Earth's SOI and enter the cruise phase on 30 November 2013.

The cruise phase is the period of travel from Earth to Mars after the spacecraft leaves Earth's SOI. Activities during the cruise phase will include monitoring of the spacecraft and science instruments, and navigation activities in order to determine and correct the flight path of the orbiter to Mars. The time taken for the spacecraft to reach Mars' SOI will be 294 days.

Two months before the spacecraft reaches Mars' SOI, the approach phase will begin. Three primary activities will take place during this phase. Navigation measurements will be taken to determine the position and trajectory of the orbiter. Trajectory correction manoeuvres will be done. Preparations will also be made for the final journey to Mars.

The scientific instruments that the MOM spacecraft carries will start working when the spacecraft is in Mars' orbit. But it is also possible to take photographs of Earth from above in the cruise phase. For about fifteen days at the start of the cruise phase, ISRO plans to image Earth. Similarly, at the end of the cruise phase, for the last two weeks, it will take images of Earth.

The spacecraft will enter Mars' SOI on 20 September 2014. The Mars Orbit Insertion manoeuvre will be carried out on 22 September 2014. At this point in the mission when the orbiter will arrive just short of Mars, small rockets will be fired to slow down the speed, and the spacecraft will get captured into a long, looping orbit around Mars. The spacecraft will need to perform a manoeuvre to slow the orbiter by about 1,109 metres per second.

Scientific instruments

ISRO had constituted a committee under the chairmanship of Professor U.R. Rao, the former Chairman, ISRO and an internationally renowned space scientist, to decide about the scientific instruments that MOM spacecraft should carry. It needs to be mentioned that Professor Rao's experiments on a number of Pioneer and Explorer spacecraft led to a complete understanding of the solar cosmic ray phenomena and the electromagnetic state of interplanetary space.

Professor Rao's committee noted that the spacecraft will be in Mars' orbit in September 2014 and will have a minimum life of ten months. The orbit of Mars is elliptical and therefore, the time that the spacecraft will get to observe Mars is limited. Because of this, it can only observe big things on Mars' surface like dust storms. The committee also noted that the mission would provide opportunities for studying Mars' atmosphere, and for observing Phobos.

The committee recommended that the scientific instruments carried by MOM spacecraft should be in three categories: Mars atmospheric studies, environment studies and surface imaging studies.

Martian Atmospheric Studies

Lympha Alpha Photometer (LAP)

This instrument will measure the presence of deuterium and hydrogen in the Martian upper atmosphere. Such measurements will allow ISRO to understand the process by which water has been lost from the planet.

Methane Sensor for Mars (MSM)

MSM is designed to measure methane in the Martian atmosphere and map its sources. MSM will give us useful information about the origin of methane and tell whether the origin is biogenic or volcanic. This instrument will take measurements of methane with an accuracy that will be much better than those achieved by space probes using image spectrometers or pressure-modulated sensors.

Plasma and Particle Environment Studies

Mars Exospheric Neutral Composition Analyser (MENCA)

This instrument will be used to understand the seasonal variations on Mars. The instrument will operate when the spacecraft is approaching Mars. A similar instrument had been flown aboard the Moon Impact Probe in Chandrayaan 1 mission.

Surface Imaging Studies

Mars Colour Camera (MCC)

The images taken by MCC will give important inputs about the features and composition of the Martian surface. The images will be useful to monitor the dynamic events and weather of Mars. The camera will also image the surface of the two moons of Mars: Phobos and Deimos MCC will image the morphology (the forms of things) of the Martian surface; it will map the morphological units, landforms, geological structures and craters; map the Martian polar ice caps and their behaviour through the seasons; observe and study events like dust storms and dust devils; and image Mars, its moons, asteroids and other celestial bodies from close quarters.

TIR Imaging Spectrometer (TIRIS)

Determining the mineralogy of Mars is the key to understanding the conditions of the surface and sub-surface. TIRIS will be useful in mapping the mineral composition of Mars using spectroscopic techniques. The data from TIRIS will also be used for studying aerosol (particles dispersed in a gas) in Martian atmosphere. On the whole, TIRIS will map the surface composition and mineralogy of Mars; detect hot spots, which indicate underground hydro thermal systems; and detect and study the variability of aerosol/dust in the Martian atmosphere.

Spacecraft Configuration

Structure

The spacecraft regulates and preserves the life of the scientific instruments it is carrying with the help of several systems and sub-systems. The structure of the spacecraft provides a strong and stable platform to house scientific instruments, systems and sub-systems of the spacecraft. While designing the structure of the MOM spacecraft, the additional consideration has been that it should protect the scientific instruments in the harsh environment surrounding Mars and provide the right conditions for the instruments to function.

The MOM spacecraft is shaped like a cuboid. The cuboid has a dimension of 1.45 metre x 1.45 metre and is 1.58 metre high. The structure is designed to provide mechanical support for all the spacecraft units and sub-systems in a configuration that meets the system requirements of a satellite.

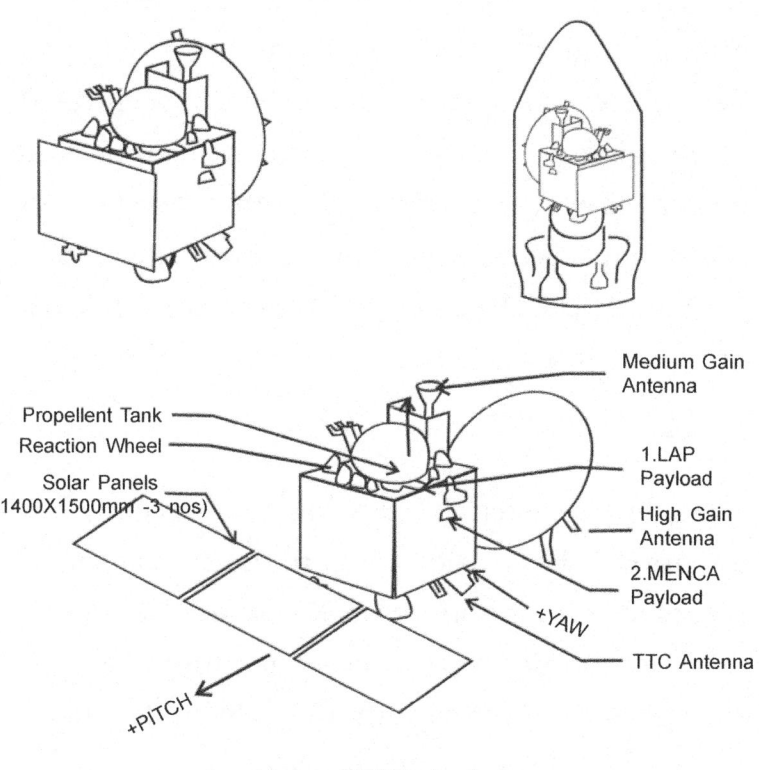

Views of MOM structure

Thermal system

The thermal system is designed to keep the temperature of the spacecraft at a comfortable level and allow scientific instruments as well as the entire spacecraft to function efficiently and safely. In addition, the thermal design for the MOM spacecraft is based on the requirements of inter-planetary cruise and Mars orbit. Thermal design for these two phases has concentrated on keeping the spacecraft warm with minimum heater power. The thermal control system of MOM spacecraft has multi-layer insulation blankets, optical solar reflectors, tapes, thermal grease, paints and coatings.

Power system

The power system of the MOM spacecraft has to support the mission in its transfer-orbit, inter-planetary cruise and on-orbit phases. The power system comprises power generation, energy storage and power conditioning elements. Power generation of the MOM consists of a single solar array that generates around 750 watts during the normal Sun incidence in Mars orbit. The storage system consists of a 36 AH lithium ion battery for powering the spacecraft during eclipse phases and downloading of data from the scientific instruments. Power electronics controls the solar array power to supply the load and charge the batteries.

Propulsion system

The basic propulsion system configuration is similar to that of Chandrayaan 1, with some modifications made to improve system safety and reliability. Two propellant tanks, each with a capacity of 390 litres and accommodating a maximum of 850 kg of propellant is adequate for the Mars mission. A liquid engine of 440N thrust is being used for orbit raising and Martian Orbit insertion. Additional flow lines and valves have been put to ensure that the liquid engine restarts after 300 days of cruise phase. There are eight 22N thrusters. The thrusters will be used for attitude control during various phases of the mission.

Attitude and Orbit Control System (AOCS)

The attitude of a spacecraft is its position in space, or its orientation. Attitude determines what a spacecraft looks at. A method used to keep the spacecraft stable and pointing in the desired direction is to stabilize it so that it does not wobble. This is done by means of three-axis stabilization by using an internal gyroscope (it is a kind of top which spins at high speed and becomes stable due to its inertia) and small rockets (thrusters).

The orbit control system makes sure that a spacecraft is in the desired orbital position and maintains that position. Such control is achieved through sensors, gyroscope and attitude actuators like reaction wheel and momentum wheel. Sometimes, it becomes necessary to make changes in the orbit. This is done by using thrusters. Thrusters are fixed on the spacecraft and on the commands from the ground station, they can be fired to control the attitude of the spacecraft.

The attitude and orbit control system of the MOM consists of a three-axis stabilized system. It also has reaction wheels to keep the spacecraft stable. Thrusters are provided to make necessary changes in the orbit.

The MOM spacecraft carries three types of sensors: Sun sensor, Star sensor and Inertial Referencing and Accelerometer Package (IRAP).

The inertial system consists of four reaction wheels while the IRAP provides information about the increases in angle and velocity.

In the MOM spacecraft, the Attitude and Orbit Control Electronics (AOCE) is the heart of the attitude control system. It provides interface with the sensors to obtain attitude information and interface with the actuators to command them to operate in a controlled manner to change the attitude of the spacecraft to the desired altitude and to maintain it.

Deployment mechanisms

The MOM spacecraft has a single solar array that is stowed but has a hold-down and release mechanism. The spacecraft also has an antenna reflector of 2.2 metre diameter to be stowed but with a reflector hold-down and release mechanism. The hold-down and release mechanisms are provided to restrain the appendages in the stowed configuration during the launch phase or till deployment. In the MOM mission, it is planned to deploy both the solar array and the reflector immediately after the injection of the spacecraft into Earth's orbit. Once deployed, the reflector will have a fixed position with respect to the body of the spacecraft and the solar array will point towards the Sun.

Telemetry, Telecommand, Tracking and Communication systems

Telemetry, telecommand, tracking and communication system has four functions. It sends information about the functioning of the spacecraft to the ground system. This is called telemetry. It conveys commands from the ground system to the spacecraft to carry out certain functions. This is called telecommand. It also supports the ground station in tracking the spacecraft. This is the tracking function. It also receives and transmits radio signals. This is the communication function.

A spacecraft needs to have some means of communication with Earth. This is necessary because the spacecraft needs to receive instructions and transmit data which it collects.

This is done by using an antenna. An antenna is a piece of equipment that allows transmission and reception of radio signals. Since information is transmitted by using radio waves, which move at the speed of light, this method allows for very fast communication.

The telemetry and telecommand configuration in the MOM spacecraft contains two packages namely TMTC-10 and TMTC-20. TMTC-10 has telecommand main system and telemetry main system, which are two separate, independent systems. TMTC-20 will provide the fall back option in case TMTC-10 does not work.

In respect of communication, the Mars mission has Telemetry, Tracking and Control (TTC) system and data transmission system. The TTC system consists of a number of antennas and feed networks. There is a Low Gain Antenna, Medium Gain Antenna, High Gain Antenna, filters and hybrids. While the Low Gain Antenna will be used for TTC application, the High Gain Antenna will be used both for TTC and data transmission application.

Deep Space Network

The Indian Deep Space Network station was established at the time of the Chandrayaan 1 mission, but it is also equipped to meet the requirements of ISRO's future missions to Mercury, Venus and Mars. The communication system, which the Indian Deep Space Network provides, supports the transmission of high and low data rate science data, housekeeping telemetry from the spacecraft to Earth, and commands from Earth to the spacecraft. Due to large variations in the range between the spacecraft and the ground stations during the life of the mission, different data rates may be used during different phases of the mission. Data can be transmitted at a higher rate when the spacecraft is nearer to Earth and at a lower rate when it is at a distance.

ISRO's Deep Space Network station has two antennas: one 18-metre (DSN 18) and one 32-metre (DSN 32). DSN 32, which is a state-of-the-art technology 32 metres Beam Wave Guide antenna, was installed to support all future deep space missions of ISRO. This antenna is capable of receiving extremely weak signals from spacecraft and probes millions of kilometres away from the ground facility using its 20kW transmitter.

DSN 32 will be used for TTC and science data collection from the Mars mission. DSN 32 is necessary because the MOM spacecraft will be far away when it is orbiting Mars, and the radio waves from the MOM spacecraft will become very weak by the time they travel the long distance to Earth. They will be so weak that it will be difficult to retrieve the valuable information they carry. That is why DSN 32 with its big dish antenna and sensitive equipment is necessary to recover the information in those radio waves after separating them from the background electronic noise.

For ISRO, planning the mission to Mars has been a great challenge. It has demanded a lot of work in planning critical mission operations and meeting the stringent requirements on propulsion and other bus systems of the spacecraft. It has also required development of sophisticated scientific instruments for conducting atmospheric studies, space plasma and particle environment studies and surface imaging studies of Mars.

The MOM spacecraft will enter the Martian orbit on 22 September 2014 and will be there in the orbit for a minimum period of ten months, studying Mars. It will give us a lot of valuable information about Mars. India will be the sixth country in the world to launch a mission to Mars after Russia, the US, Europe, Japan and China.

Chandrayaan 1 was only the beginning of India's space odyssey. With the Mars mission, ISRO would have taken us on a long, adventurous journey deep into space.

It is a long way to Mars. When it is closest to Earth, it is only 55 million kilometres away, but a spacecraft needs to travel hundreds of millions of kilometres to get to Mars. This is because the spacecraft has to follow a large curve around the Sun to reach Mars. A mission to Mars is a big challenge. By taking India to Mars, ISRO's maiden Mars mission would have done us all proud.

9
Beyond Mars

Mars will be India's stepping stone to the vast planetary world beyond Earth. ISRO is currently working on sending a probe to the Sun. As the head of our solar family, the Sun is important to us. Earth goes around the Sun at a distance that is conducive to human life. The temperature is just right to retain water as a liquid. The food chain on Earth starts with sunlight through photosynthesis. We depend on the fossil fuel created from the energy of the Sun. These are things essential for the existence of life on Earth. That is why ISRO wants to study the Sun from close quarters. It plans to send a spacecraft to the Sun soon. It will be called Aditya, and will study the Sun's corona.

ISRO is also planning a mission to an asteroid. A large number of small bodies go around the Sun in the area between Mars and Jupiter. These are called asteroids. An asteroid is nothing but a chunk of rock, and scientists believe that asteroids are the material for planets that never formed.

Vesta is a large asteroid. ISRO has chosen Vesta for its study. Scientists in ISRO are curious to learn how the Sun's family of planets and minor bodies originated. Knowledge of asteroids will help these scientists in planning ISRO's future space missions.

ISRO is also planning a Chandrayaan 2 mission. It is an advanced version of the previous Chandrayaan 1 mission to the Moon. Chandrayaan 2 will have an orbiter as well as a lander with a rover. The orbiter will orbit around the Moon and observe it from a distance. The lander with scientific instruments will soft land on the lunar surface. The rover that it will carry will be released on the surface of the Moon.

The rover will be mobile on the lunar suraface. It will carry scientific instruments which will analyse the lunar surface near the landing site. The rover will be powered with a small solar panel. It will be able to communicate with ISRO's Deep Space Network on Earth either through the communication system in the lander or the orbiter.

Made in the USA
Monee, IL
07 July 2026

56549916R00104